# Mike T

# TEN KEYS TO A HAPPY Marriage

## Relationship secrets from the book of Ruth

**Pacific Press® Publishing Association**
Nampa, Idaho
Oshawa, Ontario, Canada
www.pacificpress.com

Cover design by Eucaris L. Galicia
Inside design by Steve Lanto
Cover photo © iStockphoto.com

Unless otherwise noted, all Scripture quotations are from the HOLY BIBLE, NEW INTERNATIONAL VERSION. Copyright © 1973, 1978, 1984 International Bible Society. Used by permission of Zondervan Bible Publishers.

Scriptures quoted from NKJV are from The New King James Version, copyright © 1979, 1980, 1982, Thomas Nelson, Inc., Publishers.

Scriptures quoted from NCV are from the New Century Version, copyright © 1983, 1986, 1988 by Word Publishing, Dallas, Texas, 75039. Used by permission.

Library of Congress Cataloging-in-Publication Data

Tucker, Mike (Michael Duane)
Ten keys to a happy marriage:
relationship secrets from the book of Ruth / Mike Tucker.
p. cm.
ISBN 13: 978-0-8163-2163-6
ISBN 10: 0-8163-2163-9
1. Bible. O.T. Ruth—Criticism, interpretation, etc. 2. Marriage—religious aspects—Christianity. 3. Family—Religious aspects—Christianity. I. Title. II. Title: Ten keys to a happy marriage.
BS1315.6.M3T83 2007
248.8'44—dc22                                        2006052483

Additional copies of this book are available by calling toll-free 1-800-765-6955 or by visiting www.adventistbookcenter.com.

07 08 09 10 11 • 5 4 3 2 1

# Dedication

This book is dedicated to my wife, Gayle. She has been my life's partner for the past thirty-one years. She is the mother of my children, my partner in ministry, my companion in faith, my best friend, and the love of my life.

Gayle, thank you for modeling all of the principles in this book. Your gentle spirit and tender love have made my life sweet. Truth be known, I've learned some of these principles from you.

Now that our children are grown and we are officially "empty nesters," I can conceive of no sweeter thought than that of growing old with you. Thanks for putting up with my hectic schedule, my quirky habits, and my difficulty in ever saying no to an appointment. I love you with every fiber of my being.

Your loving husband,
Mike

**Also by Mike Tucker**

*Heart Food*

*Jesus: He's All You'll Ever Need*

*Jesus, Your Heart's Desire*

*Journal of a Lonely God*

# Contents

# Introduction

The man sitting in my office—we'll call him Kevin—was in agony. Tears were running down his face, which was contorted in pain. The pain was not primarily physical, but emotional. It was the pain of a man whose heart had been broken, whose trust violated.

The source of Kevin's pain was a marriage that was falling apart. Kevin's wife, Sally, was involved in an extramarital affair and wanted a divorce. Kevin loved Sally with all of his being. Just eleven and a half years ago, they had stood before their pastor in a church filled with family and friends as they exchanged vows of fidelity. That day seemed to have happened a million years ago on another planet.

Kevin thought about the early years with Sally. Everything was new and exciting then, and nothing was impossible. Their love was deep, fulfilling, and passionate, and it grew every day. Now those years seemed to be nothing more than a vaporous dream. It was almost as though none of it had ever happened.

Then, of course, there were the children. How would all of this affect them?

We sat in pained silence as Kevin imagined life without his precious Sally. He imagined the shock his children would experience when they learned that their lives would be ripped apart by their parents' divorce. He tried to imagine the impact the divorce would have on family finances, family reunions, Christmas celebrations, weekends, vacations, graduations, weddings, and the births of grandchildren. It was too much for Kevin to imagine. He just couldn't get his mind around all that divorce would mean.

Then Kevin's thoughts turned to the more personal effects of this tragedy. He felt the inevitable agony of rejection and the accompanying feelings of inadequacy. Kevin had to admit that at times he was embarrassed and at other times he experienced rage. A million memories filled his mind, and countless emotions flooded his heart. It was overwhelming, even paralyzing.

I broke the silence. "What are you going to do?"

Kevin hesitated for what must have felt like an eternity. Grief tightened his throat, and his racing heart vibrated his chest. Eventually, he spoke. "I'm going to fight for my marriage!" he said.

Kevin did fight for his marriage. It wasn't easy, and it didn't happen overnight, but the marriage was saved. Sally had to end the affair—something that was surprisingly difficult to do. And Kevin and Sally had to work through issues of forgiveness as they focused on rebuilding trust.

Although their marriage is stronger today than it ever was before, Kevin and Sally don't recommend that you build a strong marriage the same way they built theirs. It is better, they say, to avoid the trauma they experienced by building a quality relationship while things are peaceful.

What does it take for a relationship to last today? What is required for relationships to be meaningful and fulfilling? In a day when so many people feel disconnected and marriages fall apart before the ink is dry on the marriage license, these questions take on newfound importance. What is the secret of quality relationships?

I've never met anyone who didn't want to be loved. We all long for meaningful human relationships. It is in the quality of such relationships that we find meaning, significance, and genuine worth.

Why, then, do we find it so difficult to achieve that which we so desperately need? I believe that many people simply don't understand the basic prerequisites for lasting relationships. They don't possess the most essential foundation upon which a relationship of worth is to be built.

Components of lasting relationships can be found in the Old Testament book of Ruth. An examination of Ruth's relationships reveals that this amazing woman had not just one but perhaps several meaningful relationships. Ruth had discovered the secrets of lasting and fulfilling relationships.

In this short book, I'll attempt to outline the most basic components of lasting relationships as seen in the life of Ruth. It is my fervent prayer that the ancient story of this courageous woman will serve to strengthen your relationships.

# Section One
# Commitment

# Commitment and Security

On Valentine's Day in 2001, Mitch Hallen, an Aussie living in Britain, married his TV set! Hallen had been divorced twice—from women. In a ceremony presided over by a priest and witnessed by twelve friends, Mitch Hallen married his Sony Widescreen. He took vows of "high fidelity" and put matching gold rings on top of the TV.

When asked about this rather bizarre wedding, Mitch said that his two divorces and numerous failed romances had caused him to give up on women. He said, "My television gives me countless hours of pleasure without fussing, fighting, or backchat."

Mitch Hallen discovered what you might have learned through the years: relationships are difficult. Many people struggle their entire lives without ever really finding fulfillment in their personal relationships.

In addition to being a pastor, I'm a counselor. I can't tell you how many times I've consoled people who wonder whether it is unrealistic to believe that they could ever find a "soul mate." Many, like Mitch, have simply given up. Relationships are difficult.

In 2004, Hollywood produced a remake of a 1975 movie, *The Step-ford Wives*. It's a fictional story of men who had given up on ever having a satisfying marriage, so they found ways to take shortcuts. They found ways to, shall we say, "alter" their wives to be the women they thought they always wanted. The movie reminds us that in the real world, there are no shortcuts.

While it is true that relationships are difficult, they aren't impossible. In fact, the Bible shares principles that can make any relationship much more fulfilling and satisfying.

One place where we find these principles is in the Old Testament story of Ruth, a woman from Moab. The Old Testament book that bears her name tells a wonderful story of love from which we learn important principles of relationship. The primary relationship chronicled in Ruth is one between a woman and her daughter-in-law; however, the principles we find in this story apply across the board to every type of loving relationship.

The story is about a woman named Naomi and her daughter-in-law Ruth.

> *In the days when the judges ruled, there was a famine in the land, and a man from Bethlehem in Judah, together with his wife and two sons, went to live for a while in the country of Moab. The man's name was Elimelech, his wife's name Naomi, and the names of his two sons were Mahlon and Kilion. They were Ephrathites from Bethlehem, Judah. And they went to Moab and lived there (Ruth 1:1, 2).*

Elimelech made a decision to move his family during a time of famine. Famines were somewhat common in those days. The Israelites didn't do much by way of irrigation, so everything depended upon getting the right amounts of rain at the right times. When the rain failed, famine resulted. And since Israel was an agrarian society, the fortunes of the entire economy rose and fell on agriculture. Famines destroyed the businesses of everyone in the country—even those that were not directly associated with agriculture.

Elimelech was an Ephrathite, which meant that he was likely from a prominent family and quiet possibly had been a man of some means. Money, however, does you no good if no one has food to sell, and since the entire economy depended upon agriculture, whatever business Elimelech was involved with was certain to be in trouble. So, to improve his family's chances of surviving, he decided to move them to Moab. His plans, however, didn't pan out quite as he had hoped.

> *Now Elimelech, Naomi's husband, died, and she was left with her two sons. They married Moabite women, one named Orpah and the other Ruth. After they had lived there about ten years, both Mahlon and Kilion also died, and Naomi was left without her two sons and her husband (Ruth 1:3–5).*

First Elimelech and then his two sons died, leaving Naomi with her two daughters-in-law. This was in a day when women were without many options. They couldn't inherit their father's estate or even their husband's estate. Only men were property holders. Few women had marketable trades. If a woman's husband died, her only options were for her father, if he was still living, to take her back, or for her son, if she had one, to take her in. Otherwise, most women turned to begging, prostitution, or even suicide.

## Foreigners in a strange land

Unlike other countries, Israel had laws designed to protect the poor, so, since the famine had now lifted in Israel, Naomi decided to return home. Facing an uncertain future, she began to worry about her daughters-in-law. What would become of them? If they accompanied her to Israel, they would be foreigners in a strange land with a religion that was strange to them. They would be unmarried and poor. Naomi thought that their best chance at remarriage would be to return to their father's house, so she attempted to discourage them from traveling with her.

> *Then Naomi said to her two daughters-in-law, "Go back, each of you, to your mother's home. May the LORD show kindness to you, as you have shown to your dead and to me. May the LORD grant that each of you will find rest in the home of another husband."*
>
> *Then she kissed them and they wept aloud and said to her, "We will go back with you to your people."*

> *But Naomi said, "Return home, my daughters. Why would you come with me? Am I going to have any more sons, who could become your husbands? Return home, my daughters; I am too old to have another husband. Even if I thought there was still hope for me—even if I had a husband tonight and then gave birth to sons—would you wait until they grew up? Would you remain unmarried for them? No, my daughters. It is more bitter for me than for you, because the LORD's hand has gone out against me!"*
>
> *At this they wept again. Then Orpah kissed her mother-in-law good-by, but Ruth clung to her (Ruth 1:8–14).*

It is a real tribute to Naomi that these two young women wanted to go with her. They were willing to leave their homeland, their families, and everything that was familiar to them in order to follow her to a strange land. But Naomi urged them to return to their fathers in hopes that they would find a home and security there.

Naomi's strange statement "Am I going to have any more sons, who could become your husbands?" comes from a law in Israel. This law stated that if a man married a woman and died before he produced a son, the dead man's brother would marry his wife, and the first son from that marriage would be declared to be the dead man's son and would thus inherit the dead man's property. This is what Naomi was talking about.

After Naomi's appeal to her daughters-in-law, Orpah returned to her father's home. Ruth, however, was a different story.

> *"Look," said Naomi, "your sister-in-law is going back to her people and her gods. Go back with her."*
>
> *But Ruth replied, "Don't urge me to leave you or to turn back from you. Where you go I will go, and where you stay I will stay. Your people will be my people and your God my God. Where you die I will die, and there I will be buried. May the LORD deal with me, be it ever so severely, if anything but death separates you and me" (Ruth 1:15–17).*

Ruth refused to leave Naomi. She so identified herself with her mother-in-law that she promised to live where Naomi lived, to accept Naomi's people and her religion, and even to die where Naomi died.

The final clause, "May the LORD deal with me, be it ever so severely, if anything but death separates you and me," was very significant. Ruth was inviting God to curse her if she left Naomi. Ruth was so serious about her commitment to Naomi that she was willing to accept the curse of God in her life if she ever broke that commitment to her mother-in-law.

Very few relationships in the world today are blessed with such a high level of commitment. But such commitment is absolutely essential if a relationship is to be satisfying and fulfilling. This type of commitment says, "I will so identify myself with you that your pain will be my pain, your danger will be my danger, your enemies my enemies, until the day I die."

Mary Wilson was an army nurse during World War II. In fact, Mary was the head nurse for the Allied force that landed on Anzio beach in southern Italy. She had fifty-one nurses under her command. When the Allied forces came ashore, it was obvious that their enemies were ready for them. They were soon pinned down on the beach and faced the very real possibility of annihilation.

Mary and her nursing staff set up a hospital with tents for wounded soldiers and a tent for surgery. As Mary assisted the surgeons, bullets ripped through the tent. Eventually, the situation became so critical that the nursing staff was ordered to leave. Mary refused to go. She stayed and assisted the physicians in surgery. She ministered to the needs of soldiers recovering from their battle wounds.

Years later, while reflecting on her decision, Mary remarked, "How could I possibly leave them? I was part of them." Her commitment caused her to identify so completely with the soldiers that leaving was unthinkable.

This is the type of commitment necessary to make a relationship last through the ages. It takes a commitment of complete identification. It takes a commitment so complete that your very identity changes. It is almost as if one is saying, "I don't exist without you." Leaving is not even an option.

David Ring is an evangelist, a popular speaker, and an author. He has cerebral palsy, yet he married a beautiful woman and has fathered several healthy children. He says of his wife, "If she ever leaves me, I'm going with her!" What Ring is saying in a rather humorous way is that he has so identified himself with his wife that divorce is not an option. He is committed to that woman until death forces them apart.

Commitment is the first principle of lasting, satisfying relationships that we find in the story of Ruth. Lasting relationships begin with a rock-solid commitment to identify so completely with the other person that death is the only thing that can separate one from the other. That's what Ruth did with Naomi, and that is what is necessary for you to do if your relationships are to be lasting relationships.

## Rent-a-family

Families today are hungry for commitment. People of all ages long for the security that genuine commitment brings. But many sabotage their own happiness by claiming their supposed right to an "escape clause" if the going gets a bit too tough. As a result, most people fail ever to find even one truly satisfying relationship.

We can see an example of this problem in Japan. A Japanese entrepreneur recognized that many elderly people are finding it difficult to maintain good relationships with their own children and grandchildren. Their families are leading such busy lives that they have no time to visit. That's leaving these elderly people feeling lonely and deserted. So this entrepreneur started a very successful company to meet this need. It offers temporary relief through a "rent-a-family."

For 150,000 yen ($1,280), the Rent-a-Family company will provide three trained "stand-in family members" for three hours. Three strangers will go to the home of an elderly person and play-act as that person's children or grandchildren. Actors play the roles of children, grandchildren, daughters and sons-in-law, or whomever the client desires. Company president Karoru Inoue says that usually the actors just sit around and talk, but sometimes the clients spend time berating their pretend children for their failures to visit. Mr. Inoue says, "There are lots of old people who feel sad because everyone is chasing money and no one is paying attention to the human spirit."

One recent survey in the United States revealed that more than 40 percent of Americans admit to frequently having feelings of intense loneliness. The fact is, relationships are difficult, but without meaningful relationships, our lives are incomplete and unfulfilling.

So, the first component necessary for a relationship of genuine intimacy is rock-solid *commitment*. Ruth made a strong commitment to Naomi. Even when Naomi tried to talk Ruth into returning home, Ruth remained committed to the relationship.

> *Ruth replied, "Don't urge me to leave you or to turn back from you. Where you go I will go, and where you stay I will stay. Your people will be my people and your God my God. Where you die I will die, and there I will be buried. May the* LORD *deal with me, be it ever so severely, if anything but death separates you and me" (Ruth 1:16, 17).*

Ruth made a major commitment to Naomi. The word *commitment* is a word that many people fear. Today's generation has been described as having commitment phobia. That is exactly why so few people actually enjoy meaningful, deep, fulfilling relationships.

In Ruth's statement, we find clues as to what it means to make a commitment to a relationship. First, Ruth said, "Don't urge me to leave you or to turn back from you." Basically, she was saying, "I'm not going anywhere. I'm not running out on you, and you're going to find it very difficult to get rid of me."

When couples argue and, in the heat of battle, threaten divorce, they are destroying the fabric of their relationship. Committed couples don't threaten to leave. Instead, they promise to stand by each other no matter what the difficulty might be.

Two men were walking together through a forest when a bear rushed toward them. The man who was in front climbed the first available tree and hid himself among the leaves. The other, seeing no way out, threw himself flat upon the ground with his face in the dust.

The bear approached the prostrate man, put its muzzle close to his ear, and sniffed and sniffed. Finally, concluding that the man was dead, the bear walked away.

When the first man came down from the tree, he asked, "What did that old bear whisper to you?"

The second man replied, "He told me never to trust anyone who deserts you in a pinch."

Commitment demands solutions to problems instead of dissolution of relationships. Commitment demonstrates a willingness to stand and fight for the marriage rather than a tendency to cut and run.

When my children were small, they employed tactics used by children all over the world from the beginning of time. First, they carefully analyzed my wife, Gayle, and me in order to determine who would be most likely to give a positive response to a particular request. Then, they approached that parent in a manner designed to produce a positive outcome.

If the plan failed and parent number one denied the request, they tried plan B. They approached parent number two with the same request without revealing that parent number one had said No. It should be noted here that serious problems can arise if a parent says Yes to a request that his or her spouse has previously denied. Parent number one may become more than a little peeved at the perception that his or her authority is being undermined!

Gayle and I determined early on that we would combat our children's techniques by always remembering to ask a question before dealing with any request presented to us by our children. We would always ask, "Have you asked your mother/father?"

Our children hated this technique because it presented them with a dilemma. On the one hand, they knew that we would always support our spouse's decision. On the other, if they were to lie, they might secure a positive response to their request—however, in doing so, they would run the risk of serious consequences when the deception was discovered.

Once when my daughters came to me with a plaintive request, I asked, "Have you spoken to your mother about this?"

They looked at each other and hesitated as they grappled with the difficult choice. Then they reluctantly answered, "Yes."

"I assume she said No, or you wouldn't be asking me now," I said. "Therefore, I'll say the same thing your mother said."

"Daddy," they responded, "you always do that. Why can't you just decide?"

These were desperate times. My daughters were now grasping at straws.

"Well," I said, "one day you guys are going to grow up, get married, and leave me. But I plan to spend the rest of my life with your mother, and I'm not going to spoil that by ticking her off just to make you happy. Your mother and I are a team."

Although my daughters didn't respond with glee, I knew I had just given them a gift. I helped build security for them by reinforcing my commitment to their mother. That commitment has been the foundation of our marriage.

Ruth told Naomi, "I'm not going to run out on you. Whatever problems we may have, we will find solutions to them. I'm in this for the long haul." A lesser commitment yields a relationship with no real security.

## Shared goals

The next thing Ruth said was, "Where you go I will go, and where you stay I will stay." I believe this statement implies shared goals and dreams. " 'Where you go I will go.' We'll decide on our goals together and commit our lives to those goals. We're going to travel together in the same direction."

For almost a quarter century, one of the major goals Gayle and I have shared is that of raising a family. Now that our last child has moved out and started a life of her own, that goal is pretty well accomplished. Child rearing has, at times, been an almost all-consuming goal. It has required us to place careers, personal finances, and personal pleasure on hold so that we could focus on the bigger goal of raising our family. Although we have certainly made some personal sacrifices along the way, in no way do we regret those choices.

Reaching a major life goal that I have worked toward for half my life is one of the most fulfilling things I have ever experienced. Reaching that goal in partnership with Gayle makes the victory all the sweeter. When Gayle and I got married, we promised, "Where you go I will go, and where you stay I will stay," and we have never regretted it.

Other shared goals may include such things as financial goals, career goals, spiritual goals, and goals within the community. These are all a part of the "where you go I will go" principle of marriage.

Next, Ruth said, "Your people will be my people." When two people make the ultimate commitment of marriage, they don't marry just a woman or a man, they marry the entire family.

Arlene Tucker is my mother, but when I married Gayle Whitacre, Ethel Whitacre became my mother as well. I now have two mothers, because Gayle's people are my people. Gayle gained a new sister in my sister, Vicki; I gained two new sisters in Joni and Julie; and I gained the brother I never had in Jackson. That's what it means when we say, "Your people will be my people."

Recently, while Gayle and I were visiting her family in Tulsa, Oklahoma, for the Christmas holiday, the family secured the use of a gymnasium and engaged in a game of volleyball. Gayle's mother, Ethel, joined the game and broke her arm in a fall. When you're seventy-eight, your body doesn't deal as easily with a fall. (I guess she shouldn't have gone up against the net for a killer spike!)

Gayle and I followed the ambulance to the emergency room to care for Ethel, and we encouraged the rest of the family to stay and continue the game without us. Seeing that Ethel was in good spirits, they remained and played while Gayle and I sat with Ethel in the emergency room.

Of course, this was an inconvenience; it wasn't exactly how I would have chosen to spend precious vacation time. But when I married Gayle, I declared that her people would be my people. In this instance, it meant that I was willing to sit without complaint in a hospital waiting room while physicians treated my mother-in-law's arm. I chose to do this joyfully, as though

Ethel were my own mother. I chose to call it an honor to—in some small way—minister to the needs of Gayle's mother. That's a part of what it means to live the "your people will be my people" principle in marriage.

"Your people will be my people" also has another important application. Studies show that in successful marriages, the spouses have very few close friends who are not mutual friends. That means that if I want optimal success in marriage, the vast majority of my friends should be people whom Gayle likes too. Gayle and I may each have certain of these friends to whom we feel closer, but we should have very few close friends who are not friends of both partners.

Allow me take this one step further. If I have a close friend who interferes with my relationship with Gayle, I need to distance myself from that friend. If my close friend seems to come between my wife and me, or if my wife considers that friend a bad influence on me, I may need to place my commitment to my marriage ahead of my commitment to that friend. Exceptions to this rule occur when a partner is overly controlling and attempts to isolate his or her spouse from the outside world. But in most situations, the marriage commitment should take precedence over the friendship.

In marriage, "your people will be my people" means that we will share our lives with essentially the same people—people we have agreed upon together.

## A 90 to 95 percent success rate

Ruth also said, "Your God will be my God."

According to one researcher in the United States, we can put marriages into three basic categories. Those three categories are (1) marriages that fail and end in divorce, (2) marriages that remain intact but in which one or both partners feel unfulfilled or dissatisfied with the marriage, and (3) marriages that succeed and are mutually fulfilling and happy.

Depending on whose statistics you happen to read, category one, marriages that fail, represents anywhere from 35 to 45 percent of the marriages in the United States. Category two, marriages that don't end in divorce but aren't mutually fulfilling or happy, represents anywhere from 45 to 55 percent of all marriages in the United States. The third category, marriages that last and are mutually satisfying and fulfilling, represents only about *10 percent* of all marriages in the United States. Not a very rosy picture, is it?

Now, compare those statistics to another set of statistics. In the United States, marriages in which husband and wife share the same life-integrated faith and in which they worship together every week and pray together on nearly a daily basis report a *90 to 95 percent* success rate. These marriages last, and both partners report a high degree of fulfillment and happiness.

When Ruth said, "Your God will be my God," she was announcing a principle that is one of the most important factors in the success or failure of a marriage. In truly successful, intimate, and mutually fulfilling marriages, the partners have a shared faith. It is a faith that is based on the grace of God and integrated into their daily life. Such marriages stand a far greater chance of surviving and thriving.

To ensure the long-term happiness of your marriage, you must first commit your life to Jesus as your Lord and Savior. If you haven't married yet, you must make certain that when you choose a marriage partner, you choose someone who has made that same commitment. It will also be helpful if you are of the same denomination and if your level of commitment to Christ is similar. Marriages are much more likely to last when both partners make the commitment "*your* God will be *my* God."

The last part of Ruth's plea to Naomi contains one more important principle of commitment.

> "*Where you die I will die, and there I will be buried. May the* LORD *deal with me, be it ever so severely, if anything but death separates you and me*" (Ruth 1:17).

Ruth vowed to make her commitment to Naomi a lifelong commitment. That's the type of commitment that makes marriage work. Both parties must determine that death will be the only thing that separates them. That means that you must see to it that your behavior is such that you do absolutely nothing that would give your spouse cause to end the marriage prior to death. It also means that even if your spouse makes a mistake of such seriousness that it threatens the fabric of the marriage, your first impulse must still be to save the relationship through forgiveness and a fresh start.

*Marriage is worth fighting for!* The only way to true intimacy comes through valuing the relationship so highly that you stop at nothing to save it. When you truly value your marriage, no sacrifice that will make the relationship more secure will seem too great.

The story is told of two warring tribes in the Andes, one that lived in the lowlands and the other, high in the mountains. One day, the mountain people attacked the lowlanders, plundered their goods, and kidnapped a baby, taking the infant with them back up into the mountains.

The lowlanders didn't know how to climb the mountain. They didn't know any of the trails that the mountain people used, and they didn't know where to find the mountain people or how to track them in the steep terrain. But they sent their best party of fighting men to climb the mountain and bring the baby home.

The men tried first one method of climbing and then another. They tried one trail and then another. However, after several days of effort, they had climbed only a few hundred feet.

Feeling hopeless and helpless, the lowlander men decided that the cause was lost and prepared to return to their village below. As they were packing their gear for the descent, they saw the baby's mother walking toward them with the baby strapped to her back.

One man greeted her and then said, "We, the strongest and most able men in the village, couldn't climb this mountain. How were you able to do it?"

The woman shrugged her shoulders and said, "It wasn't your baby."

It *is* your marriage. That means that it is worth fighting for! Ruth tells us that one key component of lasting relationships is commitment. A marriage worth having is a marriage worth fighting for. It takes genuine commitment to make a marriage last.

# Commitment and Happiness

In Ruth's day, divorce was very rare. Throughout biblical times, women weren't allowed to divorce their husbands for any reason whatsoever. In cultures that allowed divorce, it was the men who had all the options and, therefore, all the power. Women were powerless to end a bad marriage.

Much has changed since biblical times. Today, in the Western world, either party can secure a divorce for almost any reason whatsoever. Committed love, a love that lasts a lifetime, seems to be nearly extinct.

Some of you will remember an old song whose lyrics stated, "I'll be loving you, always; with a love that's true, always." Perhaps you've even had those words spoken to you by someone who promised undying love for you, but somewhere along the line, "always" became "yesterday," and now love no longer exists.

Believe it or not, for some people, the pledge of an "always" love has proven to be true. Their love has weathered the years, through every trial and tribulation.

Ann Landers says that when her parents married, they had enough money for only a three-day trip fifty miles from home. However, they made a pact that each time they made love they would put a dollar in a special metal box and save it for a honeymoon in Hawaii for their fiftieth anniversary. Ann said, "My parents were always very much in love. I can remember Dad coming home and telling Mom, 'I have a dollar in my pocket,' and she would smile at him and reply, 'I know how to spend it.' "

Ann's dad was a police officer and her mother a schoolteacher, and together they raised five children. Through the years, they had their share of emergencies. But no matter how bad the emergency, they never dipped into the metal box. As the box filled, they put the money in a savings account and then bought CDs. When each of their children got married, Mom and Dad gave them a small metal box and told them their secret. All five of them began to save for their dream honeymoons.

When Ann Landers's parents reached their fiftieth anniversary, they left on their dream honeymoon. They had saved enough to provide airfare, hotel accommodations for ten days, and plenty of spending money. As they got on the plane, Ann's dad winked and said, "Tonight, we are starting an account for Cancun. That should take only about twenty-five years."

All of us long for a love like that, don't we? We all long for an "always" kind of love.

I've conducted hundreds of weddings. Not once have I ever had a couple express the desire to create a miserable home. They always plan to have a home filled with love. No one plans to live in misery. However, some of the couples whose weddings I've conducted are today living in a good deal of misery. It almost seems as if the type of committed love Naomi and Ruth displayed no longer exists.

Ruth told Naomi that she would never leave her. Even though Naomi tried to talk Ruth out of leaving her childhood home and her family, Ruth determined that she would never leave her mother-in-law. She said,

> *"Where you die I will die, and there I will be buried. May the LORD deal with me, be it ever so severely, if anything but death separates you and me" (Ruth 1:17).*

Ruth made a commitment to Naomi. She made the choice that death alone would separate them.

Why does it seem that so few actually experience committed love?

From what I've seen, I've concluded that some people head into marriage with unrealistic expectations. Some people actually think that marriage is going to make them happy. When people marry with that idea in mind, they're expecting their spouse to be responsible for their happiness. And when they're not happy, then it must be their spouse's fault. After all, making them happy is their spouse's number one responsibility!

If I truly believe that my wife should make me happy, I'll grow increasingly dissatisfied with her. I'll begin to think of ways to change her so she'll be more willing to make me happy.

Someone has said that a bride thinks of three things on her wedding day: the aisle, the altar, and him. Often, what she is actually thinking is, *"I'll alter him*—I'll make him into the kind of man who can make me happy!"

I told that little joke on a live, two-hour, worldwide broadcast on the Trinity Broadcasting Network's program *Praise the Lord.* With me on that broadcast were Billy Davis Jr. and Marilyn McCoo, formerly of the group The Fifth Dimension. We invited Billy and Marilyn to join us on the broadcast because they possess a very rare item: a show-business marriage that has endured and been fulfilling. Their marriage has survived not only the bright lights of fame but also Billy's alcoholism and Marilyn's perfectionism, among other things.

When I told my joke about what a bride thinks about on her wedding day, Billy nodded in mock approval as he nudged his wife. Marilyn admitted that it was true of her. She had worked very hard to alter Billy. She had wanted him to become more of her "ideal man," but he resisted the change.

Marilyn said that when she abandoned her efforts to change Billy and instead learned to accept him for the man he was, the marriage received a tremendous blessing. Now she thanks God for the man Billy is, and she has learned to accept and love him for being that man. She no longer tries to make him into the man she thinks will make her happy. She has chosen to be happy as she is, and more importantly, she has chosen to be happy with Billy as he is.

Marriage doesn't automatically produce happiness. In fact, if you aren't happy before you get married, it is highly unlikely that you'll be happy after marriage. Your happiness is your responsibility, not your spouse's. While it is true that we are responsible for meeting our spouse's reasonable needs, we aren't responsible for their happiness. Happiness is a choice, a decision, and no one can make that decision for you. If you choose to be happy in spite of your circumstances, it removes the pressure from your spouse to do something that is quite impossible for them to do.

## The myth of the greener grass

Here's another reason many people fail to experience happiness in marriage: the myth of the greener grass. (J. Allen Petersen has written an excellent book by that title.) Some people spend a great deal of time saying things like "If only I had married another man." "If only we had more money." "If only my wife were prettier." "If only we hadn't had so many children."

You've seen chain letters that tell you to send a dollar to everyone on the list, add your name to the bottom of the list, and in thirty days, you'll have a thousand dollars. A woman told me that she was going to start a chain letter designed to help women get better husbands. She'd have you put your name on the list and in thirty days you'd receive a thousand husbands—one of whom is bound to be better than yours!

We laugh because we often relate to "if only." But the "if only" attitude is extremely damaging to a marriage.

Naomi was Ruth's mother-in-law. I've heard mothers-in-law wish that their child had married someone more to their liking. I've listened as daughters-in-law and sons-in-law complained about their spouse's parents. Certainly, Naomi and Ruth could have engaged in such activities, but neither chose to. Instead, they chose to focus on making the relationship work.

Research demonstrates that one of the characteristics of successful marriages is that the couple engages in less "alternative monitoring" than do those with less successful marriages. In other words, when a man spends time looking at other women and wonders, "What would my life be like if I were married to her?" the marriage is in trouble. When a woman daydreams about what it would be like to be married to some other man, the marriage is headed for difficult times.

Truthfully, most people would ultimately be no happier with someone else than they are with their current partner. We know this to be true because second marriages fail at a significantly higher rate than do first marriages.

A man was taken on a tour of a mental institution. The tour guide took him to a cell where a man was beating his head against the padded walls. He kept saying, "Linda, how could you do it? Linda, how could you do it?" The guide explained that the man was in love with Linda, and when Linda jilted him, he drifted off into the ozone. He couldn't handle it.

They went to the next cell, and there was a man saying, "Linda, Linda, how could this happen? Linda, Linda."

The visitor said, "Who's he?"

The guide said, "He's the man who married Linda."

That's the myth of the greener grass.

Some marriages fail today because people tend to believe that conflict is the same as incompatibility. At the first sign of conflict, people begin to wonder whether they've married the right person. I like what the Briton said when he heard that in the United States, many people divorce because of incompatibility. He said, "I thought incompatibility was one of the purposes of marriage."

That may be true. When you take two self-willed people and bring them together, what else can you expect except incompatibility?

God wants us to grow through our incompatibilities. Conflict in marriage provides opportunity for you to experience growth in love. Healthy couples have found effective methods for resolving conflict.

It is unreasonable to believe that Naomi and Ruth never faced potential conflicts. What daughter-in-law doesn't run the risk of a run-in with her mother-in-law? Yet Naomi and Ruth apparently found a method for resolving conflict effectively. They were able to work through their difficulties to a deeper, more fulfilling relationship. So can you.

Marriages today suffer much damage because we fail to understand the nature of true love. True love is, above all, a love of *commitment*, and committed love brings happiness.

I believe God's love is based on commitment. He has committed Himself to us, and everything He does in relation to us springs out of a deep commitment. Committed love places the needs of the beloved ahead of the needs of the lover. The interests of the beloved take precedence over the interests of the lover. Certainly, it wasn't in God's best interest for Jesus to suffer and die. It was in *our* best interest. This was an act of committed love.

The decision that Jesus would die for us becomes even more incredible when we realize that the decision was made even before we had reciprocated God's love. In fact, Paul says that while we were "at enmity" with God, Jesus died for our sins.

Jesus taught us about this type of love in the Sermon on the Mount:

> "If you love those who love you, what credit is that to you? Even 'sinners' love those who love them. And if you do good to those who are good to you, what credit is that to you? Even 'sinners' do that. And if you lend to those from whom you expect repayment, what credit is that to you? Even 'sinners' lend to 'sinners,' expecting to be repaid in full. But love your enemies, do good to them, and lend to them without expecting to get anything back. Then your reward will be great, and you will be sons of the Most High, because he is kind to the ungrateful and wicked. Be merciful, just as your Father is merciful" (Luke 6:32–36).

God's commitment to love doesn't depend upon the person who is loved. It depends upon God Himself. Committed love is based on the decision of the person who loves.

It is easy to love people who are nice to us. It is easy to love people who make us feel good. Committed love, however, calls us to love on the basis of a decision to love—a decision that is independent of the behavior or attitudes of the person whom we have chosen to love.

## Love if

Some people offer a type of love that Josh McDowell and others have called "love if." "Love if" says, "I'll love you if you will do thus-and-so for me." This is a conditional love. In other words, it isn't really love—it's a malicious form of manipulation.

Others offer love that we could refer to as "love because": "I love you because you are pretty," or "I love you because you are smart," or "I love you because you are rich." "Love because" implies, "If I ever find that you're no longer pretty or smart or successful, I won't love you anymore." Again, this is conditional love, and it isn't worth having.

McDowell tells us that we should never settle for less than the best kind of love—"love period." This love says, "I have chosen to love you, period. That means that when old age and gravity do their work, I'll still love you. When I find someone who is smarter than you, I'll still love you and remain committed to you. Should the day come when you're no longer successful, I'll stay with you because I promised 'for better or for worse.' My love isn't conditional upon your doing or being anything. I have chosen to love you regardless of what you do or don't do and regardless of what you are or are not. I love you because I have chosen to love you, and I will continue to choose to love you."

You remember the words to the old country-and-western song "Release Me": "Please release me, let me go. 'Cause I don't love you anymore." Such love is "love if" or "love because," and it doesn't last. Committed love lasts because it depends, not upon the person being loved, but, rather, upon the lover. Again, we turn to the words of Jesus from the Sermon on the Mount:

> *"I tell you who hear me: Love your enemies, do good to those who hate you, bless those who curse you, pray for those who mistreat you"* (Luke 6:27, 28).

Committed love is not based on a feeling. It is not based on how pretty or smart or successful the beloved may happen to be. Committed love is based on a rock-solid decision to love. It is a love that loves regardless of whether or not we receive love in return. It rests on the decision of the lover to love.

Perhaps you are thinking that you simply aren't capable of loving that way. If so, you are right. Such love doesn't come naturally to us. Committed love is miraculous, requiring divine intervention. Committed love is God's gift.

You may feel today that your spouse is your enemy. Jesus says that you are to love your enemies. Since every divine command contains within it an implied promise of the power necessary to fulfill the command, ask Jesus to give you the kind of love it takes to love your enemy spouse. Determine that you will respond with love, meeting the legitimate needs of the one you have chosen to love. Don't do this in hope that it will change your spouse. Do it because this is how Jesus has asked you to love. Do it in obedience to Him.

If you are a husband, God is asking you to love your wife. He is asking you to love her in such a way that she will have no question but that you love her. It may mean doing whatever is necessary to answer her need for communication. God made women to desire a man who communicates with them. They need time, love, and appreciation. They need to feel needed.

I remember counseling a young woman involved in an immoral sexual relationship. She said, "It wasn't because I enjoyed that relationship so much. I just wanted to mean something to somebody."

That's the cry of many marriage partners today—both men and women. They want to mean something to somebody. Wives desire to mean something to their husbands.

The question for those of us who are married is whether we're willing to give the time, the love, and the sacrificial action necessary to recognize that our first responsibility is to our spouse. Committed lovers choose to meet their spouse's needs. They say, "I may not need this, but you need it, and I put your needs and your desires above my own." That's very difficult to do, but that's what God expects us to do for one another.

Committed lovers have a love that stands the test of time. They have a love that isn't shaken by the events of life or the ups and downs of human relationships. Since their love isn't based on feelings, it isn't capricious or temporary. Committed love is a love that endures.

Mrs. Isidor Straus and her husband were passengers aboard the *Titanic*. Mabel Bird, Mrs. Straus's maid, remembered, "When the ship began to sink, panicked women and children were the first ones loaded into lifeboats. Mr. and Mrs. Straus were calm and comforting to the passengers and helped many of them into the boats. If it had not been for them, I would have drowned. Mrs. Straus made me get into the boat and put some heavy wraps on me."

Then, Mr. Straus begged his wife to get into the lifeboat with her maid. Mrs. Straus started to get in—she had one leg over the side—but then she stepped back onto the sinking ship.

"Please, dear, get into the boat!" Mr. Straus pleaded.

Mrs. Straus looked deep into the eyes of the man with whom she'd spent most of her life, the man who had been her best friend, her heart's true companion and always a comfort to her soul. She grabbed his arm and drew his trembling body close to hers. Then she said defiantly, "No, I won't get into the boat. We've been together through a great many years. We're old now. I won't leave you. Where you go, I will go."

They were last seen standing arm in arm on the deck, the devoted wife clinging courageously to her husband and he clinging protectively to her.

Committed lovers have a love that lasts. It isn't natural for us to love this way. It takes miraculous power for mere mortals to have this kind of love. But miraculous power is exactly what God offers you today. He promises to give you the power to base your love on a rock-solid decision to love. God gave that power to Naomi, to Ruth, and to Mr. and Mrs. Straus, and He will give it to you. God will give you a love of commitment.

# Section Two
# Character

# Character and Happiness

F. B. Meyer wrote, "The supreme test of goodness is not in the greater but in the smaller incidents of our character and practice; not what we are when standing in the searchlight of public scrutiny, but when we reach the firelight flicker of our homes; not what we are when some clarion-call rings through the air, summoning us to fight for life and liberty, but our attitude when we are called to sentry-duty in the grey morning, when the watch-fire is burning low. It is impossible to be our best at the supreme moment if character is corroded and eaten into by daily inconsistency, unfaithfulness, and besetting sin."[1]

Character matters. Oscar Wilde learned this truth a bit too late in life.

A playwright, poet, and novelist, Oscar Wilde was one of the most gifted writers of his age. He was immensely gifted and was none too modest about his talent. When he arrived for a lecture tour in the United States in 1882, a customs official asked if he had anything to declare. Wilde boasted, "Only my genius."

Fifteen years later, Wilde found himself in prison on morals charges. And not long after his release from prison, Wilde died a broken man.

While in prison, Wilde wrote, "I have been a spendthrift of my genius. . . . The gods had given me almost everything. But I let myself be lured into long spells of senseless and sensual ease. . . . Tired of being on the heights, I deliberately went to the depths in search for new sensation. . . . I grew careless of the lives of others. . . . I forgot that every little action of the common day makes or unmakes character, and that therefore what one has done in the secret chamber, one has some day to cry aloud from the house-top. . . . I ended in horrible disgrace."[2]

Wilde learned that character matters and that the decisions we make every day of our lives are the building blocks of character. Contrast Wilde's life with that of Wilbur Wright.

Wilbur and his brother, Orville, are best known for carrying out the first successful heavier-than-air, manned, powered flight at Kitty Hawk in 1903. Wilbur and Orville came from a close family. Their father was a minister who, in spite of his love for his sons, had predicted that humans would never fly. His sons proved him wrong.

Wilbur died when he was just forty-five years old. His father, Bishop Milton Wright, wrote about his son's death in his diary: "May 30, 1912: This morning at 3:15, Wilbur passed away, aged 45 years, 1 month, and 14 days. A short life, full of consequences. An unfailing intellect, imperturbable temper, great self-reliance and as great modesty, seeing the right clearly, pursuing it steadily, he lived and died."

For Wilbur's father, it was not making the first successful flight that made Wilbur great but his fine character; a character that Wilbur built every day of his life by the everyday choices he made.

## More important than talent and intelligence

Employers have learned that in employees, character matters as much as do technical qualifications. An employee and an employer form a relationship of trust. If the relationship is to be mutually fulfilling, both the employing organization and the employee must possess a quality character. It is always a mistake for an employer to be drawn to the most talented or the most intelligent while ignoring issues of character.

W. Michael Blumenthal, chairman of Unisys, said this about mistakes he made in hiring employees: "In choosing people for top positions, you have to try to make sure they have a clear sense of what is right and wrong, a willingness to be truthful, the courage to say what they think and to do what they think is right, even if the politics militate against that. This is the quality that should really be at the top. I was too often impressed by the intelligence and substantive knowledge of an individual and did not always pay enough attention to the question of how honest, courageous, and good a person the individual really was."[3]

Character matters when hiring an employee, and it matters in relationships. Nothing can substitute for good character.

Herbert Spencer, the English philosopher, wrote, "Not education, but character is man's greatest need and man's greatest safeguard." Character matters. As we continue to study the book of Ruth, we find that good character emerges as another important component in lasting relationships.

The first hint we find of the importance of character is in Naomi. As you remember, Naomi and Elimelech had moved their family to Moab in an effort to escape the famine that had devastated Israel. While there, their two sons married Moabite women—Orpah and Ruth. Then all three men died, leaving Naomi, Orpah, and Ruth alone. When Naomi decided to return to Israel, both daughters-in-law volunteered to go with her. Naomi talked Orpah out of the move, but Ruth clung to Naomi and refused to leave her.

Why was Ruth willing to leave friends, family, and country and move to Israel with her mother-in-law? The only conclusion we can draw is that Naomi must have been an extraordinary woman. As a mother-in-law, no doubt Naomi had many opportunities to offend her daughters-in-law; there were many opportunities for a character flaw to raise its ugly head for the girls to see. But it appears that Naomi was the genuine article. Her character rang true.

I've seen ads for a show on television called *Bridezillas*. While I've never seen the show, I understand that it is about brides who basically "lose it" as they prepare for the wedding. Having conducted hundreds of weddings through the years of my work as a pastor, believe me, I've seen a few bridezillas! I've also seen mothers and fathers of the bride and parents of the groom who qualified as something other than truly human. That's because what we really are tends to come out when the pressure is on, and there are few more trying times in life than a wedding. At such times, character flaws stand out like neon lights.

Naomi had apparently weathered the wedding storm just fine. And she must have been a good mother-in-law after the wedding day. Mother-in-law jokes didn't arise in a vacuum, you know. Difficult mothers-in-law really do exist! Naomi, however, measured up as a woman who possessed a quality character. Her daughters-in-law loved her and didn't want to leave her.

Naomi was a woman of character. The decisions she made every day of her life had made her the woman she was. Her consistent life made her a woman whom Orpah and Ruth loved deeply. Her heart was pure—her actions showed that to be true.

It wasn't just that Naomi's behavior was right, however. There are many people whose actions are correct but who are not loved. Such a person would be what Mark Twain called "a good man in the worst sense of the word." This was not Naomi. Genuine character is not just the ability to do the right thing; it is the ability to do the right thing in the right way. The right way is always the way of love. Character is the ability to be right lovingly.

The Milton H. Berry Institute in Los Angeles was a hospital that specialized in rehabilitating polio victims and people with paralysis or other extreme handicaps. One day, the famed comedian, actor, and writer Will Rogers was entertaining patients. He had everybody laughing. Even the patients who were in the worst condition were laughing hysterically at Rogers's stories.

Suddenly, Rogers left the platform and went to the restroom. Milton Berry followed him to give him a towel, but when he opened the door, he saw Will Rogers leaning against the wall, sobbing like a child. Berry closed the door to give Rogers his privacy, and a few minutes later, Rogers appeared back on the platform, as jovial as before. No one would know that he had left the stage so he could weep for the pain of those he was there to entertain.

Rogers was doing a good thing, a "right" thing, in coming to the hospital to entertain patients. But it was a better thing that Rogers had a heart of love for those in pain. That was what made him a true man of character.

Naomi was a person with character. Not only did she do what was right, but she was also a person with a heart of love, as evidenced by the way her daughters-in-law were drawn to her.

## Another person of character

Naomi was not the only person in this story who was a person of character.

> Ruth replied, "Don't urge me to leave you or to turn back from you. Where you go I will go, and where you stay I will stay. Your people will be my people and your God my God. Where you die I will die, and there I will be buried. May the LORD deal with me, be it ever so severely, if anything but death separates you and me" (Ruth 1:16, 17).

Some people have defined character as the ability to make and keep promises. Ruth responded to the love Naomi had shown to her. Ruth's response was to promise never to leave her mother-in-law. This was a promise that Ruth kept. She cared for her mother-in-law. When the two women moved to Israel, Ruth volunteered to provide for their needs.

> Ruth the Moabitess said to Naomi, "Let me go to the fields and pick up the leftover grain behind anyone in whose eyes I find favor."
> Naomi said to her, "Go ahead, my daughter." So she went out and began to glean in the fields behind the harvesters (Ruth 2:2, 3).

Israel had laws that protected the rights of the poor. One such law was that when harvesters reaped a field, they were not to harvest the grain along the property lines. The poor were allowed to harvest this grain for their own needs. The law also stated that the poor could follow along behind the reapers and glean that which they dropped. In fact, if harvesters dropped some of the grain and moved along and then looked back and saw where they had dropped the grain, they were prohibited from returning to gather that grain. It was to be left for the poor. In turn, the gleaners were to show proper respect to the harvesters and not follow the workers too closely so they wouldn't get in their way. This was also done so that there would be no question as to whether the harvesters had left the grain or the gleaners had overstepped their boundaries.

When Naomi told Ruth of this law, Ruth volunteered to go to the fields to glean behind the harvesters. Gleaning was hot and very difficult work. The owner of the property always provided food and water for the harvesters, but gleaners had to bring their own lunch and water. And not only was gleaning difficult work, sometimes the results were disappointing.

Ruth volunteered to spare the aging Naomi not only the difficult labor but also the indignity of gleaning. Remember, Naomi had been married to Elimelech, who had likely been of a prominent family and a man of some means. Gleaning, while definitely offering Naomi the hope of survival, also suggested that she was now a poor and broken woman—something that would be hard for a woman of her age to swallow.

Naomi was all too aware of her new life circumstances. When she had arrived back in Bethlehem, she had told everyone that her station in life had changed.

> *The two women went on until they came to Bethlehem. When they arrived in Bethlehem, the whole town was stirred because of them, and the women exclaimed, "Can this be Naomi?"*
>
> *"Don't call me Naomi," she told them. "Call me Mara, because the Almighty has made my life very bitter. I went away full, but the LORD has brought me back empty. Why call me Naomi? The LORD has afflicted me; the Almighty has brought misfortune upon me"* *(Ruth 1:19–21).*

Naomi means "pleasant," and Mara means "bitter." Naomi's life was no longer pleasant, so Ruth attempted to spare Naomi the indignity of poverty by gleaning for the two of them. This type of personal sacrifice, the ability to put someone else's need ahead of your own, is a mark of true character. If you want a relationship that lasts, you must become a person of genuine character. You must become a person who makes and keeps promises, and you must become a person who genuinely loves others and places their needs above your own.

We see demonstrations of Ruth's character in her ability to make and keep the promise that only death would separate her from Naomi, in her willingness to gather food for the two women, and in her desire to spare her mother-in-law the indignity of gleaning among the poor. Ruth took it upon herself to do what she could to provide for her aging mother-in-law. She chose to glean in the fields with the poor in order that there might be grain in the house. She placed the needs and the feelings of her mother-in-law ahead of her own. In order to have a quality relationship, you must be a quality person. You must be a person of genuine character.

## The right person to marry

People have often asked me how they can find the right person to marry. My answer is that you must first *be* the right person. It is important that people spend more time and effort on becoming the right person than in seeking the right person. Character is one of the most important ingredients in establishing and maintaining quality relationships. Since Ruth and Naomi were people of good character, they were able to have a quality relationship.

If you are looking for a mate today, I encourage you to stop looking. Stop looking, and ask yourself this question: If I knew today that I would spend the rest of my life single, could I be happy? If the answer to that question is No, then do yourself and any potential mate a favor and don't get married! Don't marry until you can honestly answer the question with a resounding *Yes!*

If you couldn't live as a single person the rest of your life and be happy doing it, you are subconsciously expecting that marriage will bring you happiness. You are expecting that marriage will somehow make you complete—make you whole—and you will finally be truly happy. Forgive me for bursting your bubble, but that is utter nonsense! Marriage wasn't designed to make unhappy people happy. Marriage was intended as a means for two happy people to join their lives in the happy pursuit of a greater good.

If you are unhappy as a single, the chances are excellent that you will be unhappy as a married person. The most important characteristic of a marriageable person is the habit of happiness. Learn to be happy today—right now, while you are single. Then and only then will you be a suitable partner for marriage. And if you are already married but are not happy in that marriage, before you try to fix your mate, learn how to be happy in your present circumstances.

How do we find happiness? Allow me to direct you to a couple texts:

- *Happy are the people whose God is the LORD! (Psalm 144:15, NKJV).*

- *Happy is he who has the God of Jacob for his help,*
  *Whose hope is in the LORD his God (Psalm 146:5, NKJV).*

The best thing you can do today to begin your journey to happiness is to commit your life to Jesus. Confess your sins before Him, and allow Him to change and rearrange your life. Allow Him to develop your character. Statistics reveal that committed Christians report greater levels of happiness and contentment, and they are more likely to have a happy marriage. If you want to become a happy person, commit your life to Christ.

Once you have accepted Jesus as your Savior, you must make Him your Lord. That means that you become obedient to Him. This is the essence of character. Solomon wrote, "Where there is no revelation, the people cast off restraint; / But happy is he who keeps the law" (Proverbs 29:18, NKJV). You see, happiness is found not only in knowing God and experiencing forgiveness for sins but also in obeying God. If you would be a happy person, you must first know and obey God.

## Happiness and sex

Now, let me briefly address an area of obedience that many find diffi-cult—an area that many would rather not even discuss. The truth is, the genuine happiness that we are speaking of comes when we are obedient in *all* areas of life. Every aspect of life must be subject to God. This includes even our sexuality. A part of the principle of finding happiness through obedience to God is learning to remain sexually pure before marriage. The Bible is very clear about this—there is no mistaking God's will in this matter.

If you are married, there is only one person with whom you should be sleeping. And if you aren't married, you shouldn't be sleeping with any-one; you shouldn't engage in the "act of marriage." This act is reserved for married couples. If you are single, you are to practice abstinence. This is the clear message of Scripture—and, by the way, there are no excep-tions to this!

Purity before marriage doesn't refer just to this one specific act. There are parts of the body that members of the opposite sex shouldn't touch or see before marriage. Couples who are dating have asked me, "How far is too far?" Allow me to share a simple rule of thumb to tell you how far is too far: Any part of your body that you wouldn't feel comfortable showing to your pastor is a body part that your fiancée or anyone you date shouldn't see or touch. Leviticus 18 tells us that it is sin to view the nakedness of anyone you are not married to—even if you see that person on television or the movies. Whether you are eighteen or seventy-eight, the rule still applies. Character matters.

Some have told me, "Well, we're engaged to be married. We've talked about this and decided that since we're going to get married, it's probably all right for us to make love."

This type of thinking has so many problems that it is difficult to know where to begin to challenge it. Let me point out that one third of all en-gagements don't result in marriage. One out of three engaged couples don't end up getting married. I've seen this happen over and over again. Couples who thought they were going to get married decided that sexual activity during engagement was appropriate, but then they ended up breaking off the engagement.

In more than twenty years of counseling, I've never met anyone who decided to reserve sex for marriage and later regretted that decision. On the other hand, I've seen many people who decided to engage in sex outside of marriage and have suffered terrible regret and guilt. My wife and I were virgins when we got married. I can testify that we've never regretted that decision!

God said No for a reason. He is not some cosmic killjoy. He's the One who came up with the whole idea of sexual intimacy in the first place! What makes us think we can improve on His plan?

People tell me, "But this is the twenty-first century!" To these people I respond, "Do we really think that God's law expired at the turn of the century?" God's law has not expired. It is just as valid today as it was in the days of Jesus. It will still be valid in the next millennium. Jesus said that heaven and earth may pass away, but even then, not so much as a comma, an apostrophe, or the dotting of an *i* will be changed in God's law.

God didn't give His law to spoil your fun. He gave it so you can find happiness. "Where there is no revelation, the people cast off restraint; / but happy is he who keeps the law" (Proverbs 29:18).

I realize that what I'm saying isn't very popular today. If you are among the millions of people who borrow their morality from popular television shows or the movies, you must think I'm hopelessly out of touch with reality. But the child of God will never allow popular culture to be the determining factor in the choice of standards of personal morality. Moral choices are made on the basis of God's Word. There is no other safe course. Obedience to God is a matter of character. And character is an essential component of lasting relationships.

I remember encouraging a young man to become a man of genuine character. He told me that while he would like nothing better than to become such a person, his life was currently filled with so many hardships that he simply didn't have the luxury of developing his character. Right now, he was in survival mode.

What this young man failed to understand was that the greatest growth in character doesn't take place in times of ease. Character is formed most rapidly in times of difficulty and stress. The small, everyday choices we make in times of adversity are what make us people of depth and strength or people who are shallow. Adversity can make your character stronger.

If you take two identical acorns from the same oak tree and plant one in the middle of a dense forest and the other on a hill by itself, what do you think will happen? The oak standing on a hillside bears the brunt of every storm and gale. As a result, its roots plunge deep into the earth and spread in every direction, even wrapping themselves around giant boulders. At times, it may seem as though the tree isn't growing fast enough, but the growth is happening underground. It's as if the roots know they must protect the tree from the threatening elements. On the other hand, the acorn planted in the forest becomes a weak, frail sapling. Protected by its neighbors, it doesn't sense the need to spread its roots for support. It is too protected ever to develop as it should. Adversity makes us strong.

Nothing is said of Naomi's character before the death of her husband and sons. After this woman passed through the storms of life, Scripture portrays her as a woman of depth and strength. And Ruth lost a father-in-law and a husband. Don't you think these experiences helped these women acquire the character that we admire today?

When adversity comes your way, take care. The choices you make will have a lasting effect. Your character is being formed with every choice. As you pass through the refiner's fire, that which emerges can be pure gold.

## Purifying the gold inside

Near Cripple Creek, Colorado, gold and tellurium occur mixed as tellurite ore. The refining methods used in the early days of mining couldn't separate the two elements, so the ore was thrown into a scrap heap. Then one day, a miner mistook a lump of ore for coal and tossed it into his stove. Later, while removing ashes from the stove, he found the bottom littered with beads of pure gold. The heat had burned away the tellurium, leaving the gold in a purified state. The miner learned to extract gold from tellurite, and he made a fortune.

People are like tellurite ore. We have gold inside us, but it often takes some trial in the fiery furnace of life to transform us. It is important that in the times of stress, in our darkest hours, we recognize God's refining fire as it purifies us, producing characters of pure gold.

Christian author C. S. Lewis wrote, "Surely what a man does when he is taken off his guard is the best evidence for what sort of man he is. If there are rats in a cellar, you are most likely to see them if you go in very suddenly. But the suddenness does not create the rats; it only prevents them from hiding. In the same way, the suddenness of the provocation does not make me ill-tempered; it only shows me what an ill-tempered man I am."[4] Character matters.

Another person in our biblical story demonstrated genuine character. In Ruth 2:3, we learned that Ruth was gleaning in the field of a man named Boaz. He was a close relative of Naomi's husband, Elimelech. This is an important detail in the story.

In Israel, a law stated that if a man died before he produced offspring, his brother was to marry his widow and produce children to the dead man's name. The first son born to that relationship would inherit his father's possessions because neither a widow nor a daughter could inherit property. If the dead man had no brother, the next closest male relative was to fulfill this duty.

Boaz was a close relative, and he was single. He noticed Ruth gleaning in his field and asked one of his employees who this young woman was. He was told that she was Naomi's daughter-in-law and that she had asked for permission to glean in the field.

Ruth made an impression on Boaz. Look at what Boaz said to her:

> *Boaz said to Ruth, "My daughter, listen to me. Don't go and glean in another field and don't go away from here. Stay here with my servant girls. Watch the field where the men are harvesting, and follow along after the girls. I have told the men not to touch you. And whenever you are thirsty, go and get a drink from the water jars the men have filled."*

> *At this, she bowed down with her face to the ground. She exclaimed, "Why have I found such favor in your eyes that you notice me—a foreigner?"*
>
> *Boaz replied, "I've been told all about what you have done for your mother-in-law since the death of your husband—how you left your father and mother and your homeland and came to live with a people you did not know before" (Ruth 2:8–11).*

Boaz was a man of principle, and he was genuinely impressed by what Ruth had done for Naomi. This drew him to the young woman. There is an important lesson here. When we aspire to become a certain type of person, we are drawn to people who exhibit the characteristics we value. Character recognizes character. Boaz was a man of principle. Ruth's good character was attractive to him. Ruth's character was a more powerful aphrodisiac than a miniskirt and strong perfume. We are drawn to that which we value.

Do you know when my wife is most strongly attracted to me? She says it's when I preach. She values the Word of God, and she loves to hear it proclaimed. But she tells me that she wouldn't be attracted to me when I preach if I didn't attempt to live by the principles of God's Word. She says that the fact that I try to practice what I preach makes me irresistible to her when I preach.

So, men, please take note, because many men don't ever really get this. If you will become a man after God's own heart, you will become irresistible to the type of woman you would be proud to take home to Mom. Strength of character, especially when combined with the loving, tender spirit that accompanies genuine character, is the stuff that women are drawn to. And ladies, if you want to attract the right kind of man, become the woman God designed you to be.

By the way, the bit of advice I just gave to men is not just for single men. It's for married men as well. If you can't understand why you can't seem to get along with your wife, or if you can't understand why she doesn't give you the respect you know you deserve, or if you can't understand why she isn't romantic nearly as often as you wish she were, then this advice is for you: There is no better medicine for healing the brokenness of a bad marriage than the medicine of a godly character. A godly character will make you irresistible to your wife!

Naomi and Ruth had godly characters, and that enabled their relationship to last until death. And Ruth's godly character drew the attention of Boaz, a man of character himself, and it worked as an aphrodisiac to him.

After accepting a bit of womanly advice from Naomi, Ruth was able to spur Boaz into action. There was another relative closer than Boaz, but Boaz maneuvered himself into position to marry Ruth.

Ruth bore Boaz a son. Now Naomi's friends, the women of the town, praised God for the blessings He had poured out on her. They praised God for giving Naomi security in her old age, for giving her a grandson, and "for your daughter-in-law, who loves you and who is better to you than seven sons" (Ruth 4:15).

Seven is the perfect number in Scripture, and sons were more highly prized than daughters, so this was high praise indeed!

Are your relationships on life support? Do they seem to be drawing their last breath? Godly character could be the cure. Pray that your Lord will build in you a godly character.

---

1. F. B. Meyer, "Our Daily Walk," *Christianity Today,* vol. 36, no. 10.

2. Oscar Wilde, *De Profundis.*

3. W. Michael Blumenthal, "Candid Reflections of a Businessman in Washington: Interview With Secretary of the Treasury, W. Michael Blumenthal," *Fortune* ( January 29, 1979), 36–49.

4. C. S. Lewis, *Mere Christianity* (London: Geoffery Bles, 1952), 192.

# Character and Dating

Young people today face a challenge that Ruth and Boaz never even dreamed about. They face the challenge of dating.

Dating is a fairly recent sociological phenomenon. It's been around in the Western world for only a little more than a hundred years. Even today, dating is unheard of in many parts of the world.

Ultimately, dating has one major function: People date to find a mate. While dating can serve several other functions, such as having fun, developing social skills, and learning about the opposite sex, its main value lies in mate selection. However, if the divorce rate in the West is any indicator, dating has failed miserably at fulfilling this purpose.

Arranged marriages were the order of the day in Ruth's day. It's likely that most marriages in the world today are arranged marriages too. Several couples in my church have marriages that were arranged in the countries of their birth. They seem to do at least as well as those marriages that came about by dating.

Ruth and Boaz didn't date. Their marriage came about through circumstances that were unusual even for their day. Ruth was from Moab, and she was a widow. Boaz was an older man. We don't know whether he'd been married before, but it's likely that he had been since marriage and producing offspring were thought to be the solemn duty of every man in Israel. If Boaz had been married previously, it is likely that he, too, had been widowed, since divorce was almost unheard of in that day.

Ordinarily, the parents of the couple would have gotten together and agreed that their children should be married. Once they struck the deal, they would announce the betrothal to the community and set a date for the wedding. But Ruth and Boaz had no parents who could arrange for their marriage, so another way had to be found. Somehow, they had to begin a courtship and then produce a marriage.

Ruth and Boaz had a rather strange courtship. Ruth met Boaz as she gleaned in his field. Boaz found Ruth attractive and made inquiries about her. He liked the things he learned, so he made overtures of kindness toward her.

When Naomi learned of Boaz's interest, she informed Ruth of the law regarding the close kinsman. This law stated that if a man of Israel died before producing offspring, a near kinsman was to marry the dead man's widow and father a son for him. The dead man's inheritance would belong to the first son born of the union between the near kinsman and the widow. This was done so the dead man's name wouldn't be erased from the land. Since only males could inherit land, the family's ancestral land would pass from that family if there were no male heir. Therefore, the law of the near kinsman helped keep the family farm in the family.

Naomi told Ruth about this law. Ruth immediately saw its value to herself and to her mother-in-law. Boaz could marry Ruth, redeem the land that had belonged to Elimelech, and thus end the two women's poverty.

Naomi then shared a strange ritual with Ruth. We don't find it anywhere else in Scripture, so we know next to nothing about it. We'll give closer attention to this ritual in a later chapter, but for now, let's look at the passage that tells us how Ruth snagged her husband. As background, remember that Ruth went to the threshing floor one evening after the harvest was over and waited for her opportunity.

> *When Boaz had finished eating and drinking and was in good spirits, he went over to lie down at the far end of the grain pile. Ruth approached quietly, uncovered his feet and lay down. In the middle*

*of the night something startled the man, and he turned and discovered a woman lying at his feet.*

*"Who are you?" he asked.*

*"I am your servant Ruth," she said. "Spread the corner of your garment over me, since you are a kinsman-redeemer."*

*"The LORD bless you, my daughter," he replied. "This kindness is greater than that which you showed earlier: You have not run after the younger men, whether rich or poor. And now, my daughter, don't be afraid. I will do for you all you ask. All my fellow townsmen know that you are a woman of noble character. Although it is true that I am near of kin, there is a kinsman-redeemer nearer than I. Stay here for the night, and in the morning if he wants to redeem, good; let him redeem. But if he is not willing, as surely as the LORD lives I will do it. Lie here until morning."*

*So she lay at his feet until morning, but got up before anyone could be recognized; and he said, "Don't let it be known that a woman came to the threshing floor" (Ruth 3:7–14).*

That's it! A little different from dinner and a movie, but it was effective nonetheless. However, I wouldn't recommend that you attempt the threshing-floor routine to find a mate. And since I don't see arranged marriages making a comeback anytime soon in the West, you may have to go through the dating ritual to find someone to marry.

However, be aware that dating is fraught with peril. The practice holds many traps that are very easy to fall into, so allow me to share a few suggestions.

## For a successful courtship . . .

1. Make certain that you date only people of genuinely good character. You will eventually marry someone from the circle of people whom you date. It is better to play it safe here—date only potential candidates for marriage. Date only people of genuinely good character. It's a mistake to assume that character can develop after marriage. Wait to see the genuine article first; then you can consider marriage.

2. It is also wise to date only those who meet your minimum requirements for a marriage partner. If you don't have a list of the qualities your marriage partner absolutely must have, I suggest that you create one. Here's a list you might consider when making up your own:

## Qualities of a Potential Marriage Partner

☐ Someone who is a committed Christian of my denomination
☐ Someone with whom I find it easy and fun to have a relationship
☐ Someone who doesn't abuse alcohol, drugs, or other harmful substances
☐ Someone who isn't physically or verbally abusive
☐ Someone who doesn't have a history of violence
☐ Someone with a positive self-image
☐ Someone whose likes, dislikes, interests, and values are similar to my own

This list of minimum requirements for a marriage partner is a good place to start. You may have other requirements. I could certainly come up with a few more of my own!

Once you've compiled your list, it is important to make certain that you date only people who meet those minimum requirements. Since it's difficult to know all these things about a person before the first date, you'll need to be constantly reevaluating as you date. If, after a few dates, you find that the person you're dating doesn't meet one of your minimum requirements (any one of them), you must break off the relationship immediately! This is key. Continuing to date someone who doesn't meet the nonnegotiable minimum requirements to be your marriage partner is dangerous. You run the risk of developing a strong attachment to this person. Such an attachment could cloud your judgment and cause you to marry someone who, if you weren't wearing the rose-tinted glasses that romance supplies, you would never consider as a marriage partner.

Allow me to repeat this very important point: Consider every item on your list of minimum requirements absolutely essential. Even if the person you're dating meets all of them but one, break up today! This is not negotiable. Believe me, after thirty years of marriage counseling, I can name scores of couples who wish they'd known and followed this bit of advice when they were dating. Their failure to do so has resulted in a miserable existence and even in divorce. How much better would it have been to endure the pain of the breakup of a dating relationship than to live in marital purgatory or to endure the torture of a divorce!

3. Here's another suggestion for dating: Date only those people who respect your value system. It is important that people know that you value purity and that the people you date respect that value system.

A young woman came to me in tears. She told me that her boyfriend, whom she loved deeply, was pressuring her for sex. He knew what her values were, but he insisted that everyone was "doing it" and that he needed it in order to continue in the relationship.

This young woman was struggling with the decision either to violate her values and keep her boyfriend or to keep her values and be rejected by her boyfriend. You can guess which choice I urged her to make!

The boyfriend was offering his girlfriend conditional love— the "love if" kind of love we discussed in chapter 2. He was saying, "I'll love you if you'll have sex with me."

"Love period" is the only kind of love worth having. And anyone who refuses to honor your standards doesn't love you with "love period." If you want true love, you must break off relationships with people like that!

A woman in her twenties told me that her boyfriend attempted to get her to violate her value system by saying, "If you loved me, you'd let me!" She said she replied, "If you loved me, you wouldn't pressure me to do something I view as a sin before my God." Wow! That takes courage! I was so very proud of her. This woman's courage will pay dividends in the years to come.

So, make a firm decision to date only those who will respect your value system. Failure to do so could have disastrous results.

4. When you choose someone to date, attempt to engage in dating

activities that allow for conversation. This will help you to get to know each other.

Those who go to a movie theater and call it a date have failed to provide opportunities for interaction. Concerts, plays, and other spectator events can also make carrying on a conversation difficult if not impossible. While I wouldn't say that you should never have this type of date, just remember that the ultimate goal of dating is to find a person of character. If you don't get to know the person, you'll never know anything about his or her character. Dates that allow for interaction provide opportunities to make discoveries about the values, beliefs, goals, and integrity of the person you are with. Make this a priority.

If you live in the West, chances are no one will arrange a marriage for you. And I don't know any obscure threshing-floor rituals that might assist you in finding a life partner. Dating may be your only option. If so, at least date intelligently. Choose to do so in a manner that will provide you with the best chance of success—success meaning that you've found someone with whom you could live "happily ever after"!

# Character and Forgiveness

Lynn Swann played football for the Pittsburgh Steelers. His illustrious career included Super Bowl wins and Pro Bowl appearances. After his career was over, Swann was voted into the National Football League's Hall of Fame. Induction into the Hall of Fame recognizes a player as one of the best to have ever played the game; Swann had reached the pinnacle of success for his career.

During the induction ceremonies, Swann expressed some feelings that had been on his mind for a long time. He harbored feelings of resentment against a former teammate, quarterback Terry Bradshaw.

In his book *Keep It Simple*, Bradshaw said Swann blamed him for Swann's not being voted into the Hall of Fame sooner. Bradshaw quotes Swann as saying, "Bradshaw did not seem like he wanted to throw the ball in my direction. He has four Super Bowl rings . . . but could he read secondaries? I doubt it. What made Bradshaw decide not to throw more passes at the end of my career, I have no idea, no idea."

Bradshaw commented, "I kept thinking how sad it was that he chose what should have been one of the greatest days of his life to create this controversy. Why let the past spoil such a wonderful day? Instead of using that opportunity to release some anger, he should have enjoyed all the honors due him. He should have been thrilled."

Few things can destroy relationships like resentment. This emotion takes the joy out of life and makes lasting relationships impossible.

The antidote to resentment is forgiveness. Yet, while it is easy to say that forgiveness is necessary, forgiving someone who has hurt you isn't an easy thing to do. It's especially difficult if the person who hurt you is someone close to you, and who could be closer than a spouse?

Many have told me that they don't think forgiveness is difficult—they think it is impossible! They tell me they simply don't have it within themselves to forgive those who offend them. When people tell me this, I remind them that without forgiveness no one can live in harmony with anyone for long since, if given enough time, everyone will offend at some point. Forgiveness is a mark of character. Only people of genuine character are capable of forgiving those who cause them pain.

The author of Hebrews tells us that we are to live in peace with each other. "Make every effort to live in peace with all men and to be holy; without holiness no one will see the Lord. See to it that no one misses the grace of God and that no bitter root grows up to cause trouble and defile many" (Hebrews 12:14, 15). This implies that we absolutely must learn to forgive each other.

Notice that in verse fourteen, Paul says that we are to "live in peace with all men and to be holy." Other versions say "sanctified" where the New International Version says "holy." In either case, this verse reminds us of the Old Testament writers' constant calls for God's people to be holy or sanctified.

The Hebrew word that is translated as "sanctified" is used in association with marriage. When two people come together in the committed, intimate relationship we know as marriage, they are "sanctified." In other words, the two were dedicated to the deepest human intimacy that can be known on this earth. So, when the Old Testament writers called Israel to be holy or sanctified, the primary emphasis was not on behavior but on relationship. By employing the word *sanctified,* the Old Testament prophets were calling Israel to a relationship of the deepest commitment and intimacy imaginable—an intimacy similar to the relationship of committed marriage. And as people responded to the call to holiness, their behavior changed—not because they focused on the behavior but because of their relationship with God. The prophets' call to holiness was primarily a call to a committed, intimate relationship with God.

Some New Testament scholars suggest that while the New Testament was written in Greek, not Hebrew, the majority of the New Testament authors were Jews who were steeped in a Jewish understanding of spiritual things. This is especially true of the author of the book of Hebrews, a book written to Jewish Christians from a Hebrew perspective. Therefore, when the New Testament writers call people to live a holy or sanctified life, the emphasis isn't primarily on behavior; rather, it's on a deeply committed, intimate relationship with God—a relationship best illustrated by the human relationship of marriage.

In fact, Paul often used marriage to illustrate Christians' relationship with God. So it's not a stretch at all to suggest that Paul is focusing on relationship issues rather than behavioral issues when he calls us to live holy or sanctified lives. Paul repeatedly states the obvious—that without such a deeply committed and intimate relationship, "no one will see the Lord." You won't see Him today in your daily life, and you won't see Him when He comes again to claim His own.

## Grace—God's free gift

How can sinful creatures enter into such a relationship of commitment and intimacy with a holy God? That is the work of grace. It's what the gospel is all about. It's the story of a holy God who longed for reconciliation with a creation whose sin had alienated it from His presence. In order to bridge the gap, Jesus, the Son of God, became "flesh and dwelt among us." He lived a holy life—perfectly holy—and paid the penalty for our sins, thus paving the way for reconciliation with the Father. The life, suffering, and death of Jesus make possible the committed, intimate relationship necessary if we are to see the Lord.

To top it off, God gives the reconciliation won by His Son as an absolutely free gift to anyone who believes in Jesus as the Son of God.

Paul writes, "If you confess with your mouth, 'Jesus is Lord,' and believe in your heart that God raised him from the dead, you will be saved. For it is with your heart that you believe and are justified, and it is with your mouth that you confess and are saved. As the Scripture says, 'Anyone who trusts in him will never be put to shame' " (Romans 10:9–11).

Making such a confession of your belief in Jesus as the resurrected Lord guarantees you the gift of eternal life. The emphasis isn't on behavior; it's on the unmerited grace of our holy God! You are loved, accepted, and forgiven just as you are today!

We see a pattern in Paul's writings. First, Paul felt that the grace of God was the most important thing in the world, and so he shared it with everyone he met. In Paul's mind, the relationship of saving grace was the most important thing in the universe.

Then, once people had received the grace of God, Paul began to explain what it meant to live as a person who was saved by grace. He described the behavioral changes that a person who answered the call to holiness would make—that deeply committed, intimate relationship with God made possible by His grace.

Notice that first comes the loving relationship and then come the behavioral changes. This is always the proper pattern. Placing the priority on the behavior produces legalism, which destroys intimacy in relationships.

We find another example of this in Colossians. In chapters 1 and 2, Paul shares the grace that comes through the death of Christ on Calvary's tree. Then, in chapter three, he says, "Therefore, as God's chosen people, holy and dearly loved, clothe yourselves with compassion, kindness, humility, gentleness and patience. Bear with each other and forgive whatever grievances you may have against one another. Forgive as the Lord forgave you. And over all these virtues put on love, which binds them all together in perfect unity" (Colossians 3:12–14).

Paul is saying, "You've received grace. Now allow that grace to change your life. Allow it to change your behavior, your attitudes, your values, and your relationships. Allow the grace of God to change you into a compassionate, kind, humble, gentle, patient, and forgiving person. These are the marks of intimacy with Christ. These are the signs that a person possesses genuine character."

Do you realize just how freeing the grace of God is? When you learn that the Creator-God of the universe loves, accepts, and forgives you just as you are, when you learn that this same God so deeply longs for intimacy with you that He was willing to sacrifice His Son to obtain it, then you are freed to love and accept others. The grace of God frees you to make the behavioral and attitudinal changes necessary for you to become a desirable marriage partner.

It has been my observation that this is exactly what grace does. When people finally get it, when they finally understand what God has given them in the incredible gift of grace through His Son, something happens inside. Healing occurs. The grace of God changes everything.

There is power in God's grace—power that we often underestimate. I am a trained counselor, but I freely admit that I find in grace a power that eclipses all my training, skills, techniques, and professional experience. God's grace gives Christian counselors something to offer that secular counselors cannot offer. As a counselor and pastor, I take the command of Hebrews 12 seriously: "See to it that no one misses the grace of God" (verse 15). "No one!" Everyone is to experience the healing, transforming power of the grace of God.

## Bill and Sue

I remember a couple I was working with whose marriage seemed to be dead. Years earlier, she—we'll call her Sue—had an affair. While nothing excuses an affair, I knew why Sue had been susceptible. Her husband—we'll call him Bill—was a rigid, legalistic, demanding, and controlling man. His cold demeanor pushed Sue away, right into the arms of another man.

After Bill found out about the affair, he said he forgave Sue. But in his heart, he hadn't forgiven her at all. As the years passed, his bitterness grew until finally he decided that he would get even. Bill set out to have an affair of his own, and he was successful.

Sue realized that something was going on with Bill. She noticed how he was relating to a mutual friend at church, so she confronted Bill. He said that he was just good friends with the woman and denied that anything inappropriate was happening; however, he agreed to come to counseling. As the sessions continued, he slowly admitted to bits and pieces of inappropriate behavior. However, the cold, legalistic front he wore wouldn't allow him to become vulnerable.

As a part of our work together, I assigned Bill some reading. I asked him to read a book that had nothing to do with marriage but dealt with the grace of God. Bill was puzzled as to why I would have him read such a book, but he agreed anyway. As he read the book, the Holy Spirit began to work in his life.

Soon, Bill admitted the true nature of his relationship with the other woman and asked for Sue's forgiveness. He forgave her for her previous affair and began to make changes in their relationship. Sue didn't know the reason for the sudden change in Bill's demeanor, but she was certainly thrilled about it! She felt like she was living with a totally different man.

However, after so many years of living in an unsatisfying marriage, Sue was understandably reluctant to believe that the changes would last. They seemed too good to be true. Sue found herself always waiting for the other shoe to drop and so held back from experiencing the fullness of joy in her marriage.

One evening as we met together, Sue confessed her fears. She asked, "How can I know for sure that the changes will last?" I turned to Bill and asked, "Bill, what can you tell your wife to reassure her?"

Bill hesitated, and as he paused, I saw that there were tears in his eyes. I said, "Bill, you've experienced a conversion, haven't you!" Bill began to nod his head. He said, "Now that I've found the grace of God, I can never go back to being the man I was before. I will never be the same."

As a reminder of the grace Bill and Sue had experienced, we had a Communion service in my office. We used the symbols that Jesus left with His church—water, bread, and wine. Bill and Sue washed each other's feet as I shared Scripture with them and spoke of the significance of what they were doing. Then they partook of the sacred emblems—symbols of the broken body and shed blood of Jesus. Bill and Sue experienced anew the cleansing power of the grace of God by accepting the sacrifice of Christ, and they embraced with hot tears of repentance and forgiveness. It was a holy moment; we were standing on holy ground. So thick was the presence of the Spirit and so intimate was that moment that I realized that I was an intruder, and I excused myself, leaving the couple to experience the sacredness of that moment alone together.

I wish you could see this couple today. After more than twenty years of marriage, Bill and Sue look like newlyweds! God's grace has changed their marriage forever.

Forgiveness can be very difficult. When a marriage has been violated by an affair, the resulting breach of trust is not easily repaired. Most of us find that we can't accomplish the task alone. Because forgiveness is not a natural act, we need help.

## A four-part plan for forgiving

Allow me to share with you a four-part plan that I've borrowed from Lewis Smeeds. I've altered his plan, which is biblically based, just a bit. This plan has helped countless people find relief from the bondage of resentment.

The four parts of this plan are *hurt, hate, heal,* and *harmony.* When people work each of the four steps thoroughly, I've found that by God's grace, even the most heinous wrongs can be forgiven. The entire process may take weeks or even months to complete. Remember that being involved in the active process of forgiving is as important as the actual forgiveness. Don't think that you must forgive immediately, especially when the offense is great and the damage severe. When you are involved in the process, how long the process takes often becomes unimportant.

I encourage people to write a letter or make journal entries with each of the four steps. Putting everything down on paper is an important part of the plan. As we walk through the four steps, I will illustrate each one from the perspective of someone who needs to forgive a spouse for an extramarital affair.

The first step of the plan is *hurt*. In this step, we ask the question What was done to me, and how has it affected my life?

The obvious thing that was done has to do with the affair itself. The effects of the affair are many. Through years of counseling with people who are attempting to work through the nightmare of an extramarital affair, I've learned that the offended party often feels betrayal, rejection, a violation of trust, and even a sense of inadequacy or worthlessness. They begin to question their judgment either for having chosen to marry someone who would do such a thing or for making choices in the relationship that may have contributed to the affair. If they were unaware that the marriage was in such bad shape that an affair could occur, they feel foolish.

If your spouse has been unfaithful, you know that your life has been forever changed. You have experienced the death of your dream of having a quality marriage. You now question yourself and your mate. You may become suspicious of everything your spouse does or says. You worry about sexually transmitted diseases, and if you're a woman, you may even worry about whether the other woman will become pregnant. If you have children, you're also concerned about how the affair will affect them, and you wonder how your spouse could do this to the children you share. All of this and more are included in the hurt caused by the affair, and you must acknowledge every pain caused by the offense.

The second step is *hate*. Harsh though it sounds, this step deals with the negative emotions we feel toward the person who has harmed us. During this step, we ask the questions Who did this to me, and how do I feel about that person?

In the case of an extramarital affair, the answer to the "who" question may not be as clear-cut as you might think. Certainly, the spouse is the one who caused harm. The spouse's lover also fits this category. And some people feel a great deal of personal guilt for the poor quality of relationship that led to the affair, so they may need to forgive themselves as well. For now, we'll focus on the offending party, although each person, including the one suffering the hurt, may need to be taken through each of the four steps.

How does a person feel about his or her spouse after an affair? The answer to that question varies from person to person. Many people have used words like *angry, disappointed,* and *hateful* when describing their feelings toward the offending spouse. Others acknowledge that they still love their spouse and find that no one word adequately describes how they feel. Often it is helpful for the offended party to express his or her feelings by saying, "A part of me really hates you, while another part still loves you." In this way, feelings can be more accurately expressed.

The third step is *heal.* Once you have identified what you are forgiving someone for and exactly who it is that you are forgiving, you must decide what you are going to do with all that knowledge. The question to ask with this step is, Now that I know answers to the "what" and the "who" questions, what am I going to do? The only answer available to a Christian is to forgive.

Forgiveness is not an emotion. Forgiveness is a conscious choice. We choose to lay aside the resentment we feel toward another person.

It is important to know what forgiveness isn't. Forgiveness isn't saying that what was done to you wasn't wrong or that it doesn't matter. It was terribly wrong, and it does matter! Forgiveness says that you refuse to carry the terrible load of resentment, anger, and bitterness that you once carried for the offending party. It is a decision to cancel the debt or to cover the offense. But forgiveness is not forgetting. God never asks us to forget the offenses committed against us. Only God can completely forget sins He has forgiven.

Some offenses are so great that they seem impossible to forgive. For these offenses, I have found it helpful simply to borrow the forgiveness of Jesus until He gives me the ability to forgive.

Corrie ten Boom and her family secretly housed Jews in their home during the Second World War. Their "illegal" activity was discovered, and Corrie and her sister Bessie were sent to the German death camp Ravensbruck. There, Corrie watched many people, including her sister, die.

In 1947, Corrie returned to Germany to preach forgiveness. Her message was, "When we confess our sins, God casts them into the deepest ocean, gone forever. And even though I cannot find a scripture for it, I believe God then places a sign out there that says 'No Fishing Allowed.' "

On one occasion, in the middle of a sermon, Corrie spotted someone she recognized in the congregation. After the message, the man she recognized pushed his way toward her. He had been guard number 8212, one of the cruelest guards in Ravensbruck. Corrie and her sister Bessie had suffered terribly at his hand.

Guard number 8212 reached Corrie, thrust out his hand, and said, "A fine message, Fraulein! How good it is to know that, as you say, all our sins are at the bottom of the sea!"

Corrie remembered all the atrocities committed by this man. She remembered her sister who had suffered and died in that cruel place of torture. Her blood froze, and she couldn't shake the man's hand.

The man spoke again. "You mentioned Ravensbruck in your talk. I was a guard there. But since that time, I have become a Christian. I know that God has forgiven me for the cruel things I did there, but I would like to hear it from your lips as well. Fraulein, will you forgive me?"

The last thing Corrie wanted to do was to forgive this man, but she remembered the words of Jesus, "If you do not forgive men their trespasses, neither will your Father in heaven forgive your trespasses." So, she prayed silently, "Jesus, help me! I can lift my hand. I can do that much. You supply the feeling."

Corrie wrote, "So, woodenly, mechanically, I thrust out my hand into the one stretched out to me. . . . As I did, an incredible thing took place. The current started in my shoulder, raced down my arm, sprang into our joined hands. . . . Then this healing warmth seemed to flood my whole being, bringing tears to my eyes." And Corrie cried, "I forgive you, brother! With all my heart!"

Corrie knew that she didn't have the power to forgive this man. It seemed that she had borrowed the forgiveness of Jesus for him until the Holy Spirit gave her the gift of her own feelings of forgiveness.

When you decide to forgive, write a letter of forgiveness. Include in the letter the precise offense you are forgiving. Include the negative effects of the offense that you are forgiving as well. Then write the words *I forgive you.* Once you have written the letter, read it aloud to the offending party. As I mentioned before, I often will lead the couple in using the symbols of forgiveness given to us by Jesus—wine, bread, and water. Just as Jesus washed the feet of His disciples, the couple washes each other's feet. Then they partake of Communion as I read Scripture and explain what the service means. We close with a prayer. This ordinance serves as a tangible reminder of what Jesus has done for us. The physical experience of foot washing and Communion helps cement the decision to forgive.

The last step of the plan is *harmony.* Once the decision has been made to forgive, the only question that remains is, How will I treat this person now? In many cases, it is important to choose to treat the offending party as though they had never sinned against you. This is how Jesus treats us when we have sinned and been forgiven. For humans, however, trust must be rebuilt before the relationship can return to some level of normalcy. Trust is extremely fragile and can often take some time to rebuild. Because it is earned, it can be restored only as, over time, one proves to be worthy of trust.

In other cases, it is important that the relationship never return to one of intimacy and trust. In cases of abuse in which the abuser is likely to re-offend, it may be unwise ever to resume a close relationship. It may even be unwise to have any contact at all with the abuser. This doesn't mean you haven't forgiven the offender. One can forgive completely and yet decide that any continued relationship would be unsafe.

However, while you may not need to resume a close relationship, forgiveness is not optional. Scripture commands us to forgive. We are to give to those who offend against us the same grace that God extends to us when we offend Him. Scripture says, "See to it that no one misses the grace of God" (Hebrews 12:15). Why? Because grace changes everything! Grace changes us! There is power in the grace of God.

## John and Naomi's story

I've seen grace make miraculous changes in the counseling office—changes so dramatic, sudden, and complete that I knew for certain that my skills as a counselor didn't produce them. It was the miraculous power of grace to change lives that made the difference. When a life is changed by grace, when a person enters a committed, intimate relationship with God, genuine healing occurs, and behavioral changes almost always follow as a natural course of events. Allow me to illustrate.

Some years ago, I performed a wedding for a young couple I knew well. However, I had some doubts as to whether their marriage would be successful. John was a linear, logical thinker. He had little use for emotions and was rigid and inflexible, dogmatic, highly controlling, angry, and worst of all, a hard-core legalist. Like most hard-core legalists, John's heart held little room to accommodate failure. He couldn't tolerate any deviation from what he thought to be the norm.

Naomi, on the other hand, was a nonlinear thinker. She wasn't structured and certainly not rigid or inflexible. Life was one happy adventure for her. She was feelings-oriented and relationally motivated. Naomi had a living, loving relationship with God that celebrated His unconditional acceptance for her. She desired a similar relationship with John and expected that eventually he would change and become the loving, accepting man she desired.

The couple hadn't been married long when John's controlling, legalistic, and rigid nature began to crush Naomi. She resisted being controlled, though, and the disapproval and condemnation she felt from John slowly destroyed her love for him. After ten long, hard years of marriage, Naomi told John that if he didn't come with her to counseling, the marriage was over. So John came with Naomi to see me.

All the sessions were painful. Invariably, they seemed to come back to something John was doing to destroy his wife's love for him. John and

Naomi were making little progress, and Naomi was making plans to leave him very soon. About that time, John made the following statement at one of our sessions: "I come here every week to take my beating. I know Pastor Tucker has ideas about marriage that are very liberal—much more liberal than mine—but I come here to take the beating in hopes that it will make my wife happy."

The argumentative side of me wanted to confront John on this issue of my "liberal ideas" about marriage, but I let it go. We quickly finished the session and made plans to meet again the next week.

John is a firefighter. During that week, he took his Bible and some books on marriage by a Christian author with him to the fire station where he worked so he could study marriage and prove that I was wrong. When he showed up with Naomi for their next session, he was carrying one of those marriage books in his hand.

Now I love the writings of this particular author, but I've been a pastor long enough to know that it isn't usually a good sign when someone who disagrees with you comes to a meeting armed with a book. It usually means that you are facing a battle, and sometimes a dirty one.

When we sat down, John asked if he might begin the session by reading a few things from the book. I said, "It's your session. Go ahead."

When John began to read the first passage he'd selected, I thought, *Are you listening to what you're reading? That's exactly what I've counseled you!*

At the end of the passage, John said, "This author told me not to do this, but I've done it. And in so doing, I've destroyed my wife's love for me."

He then went to the next passage, and as he read, I realized that he was reading something that agreed exactly with what I had told him. The same thing was true with the third and fourth passages. After about the fifth passage, I couldn't help myself. I said, "That author sure has some liberal ideas about marriage!" Naomi roared with laughter, and even John had to laugh and say, "You just couldn't wait to get me back, could you?"

John continued reading until he had finished seven or eight passages. Then he said, "Everything she told me not to do, I've done, and in so doing I've damaged my wife and destroyed her love for me." Then John got down on his knees, took Naomi's hands in his, and said, "I've seen that I was wrong. I've been introduced to the grace of God this past week, and God has forgiven me. Will you please forgive me and give me another chance?"

Hot tears of repentance and forgiveness filled the room. The Holy Spirit was obviously present in His fullness, and I was left with the strange but wonderful awareness that my degree in counseling, my training, my skills, and all my years of experience had failed to accomplish what God had done through the power of grace!

The word *grace* is simply shorthand for the gospel. The gospel is the basic tenet of Christianity. It declares that Jesus died for the guilty so He could pay the penalty for their sin and offer to them the life that only He deserves—eternal life—as a free gift. There is nothing that anyone can do to earn or deserve it. It is a gift from the hand of our gracious God. This is the gospel. This is the source of grace for our life.

When God forgives our sin, He buries that sin at the bottom of the sea. At its deepest, the ocean bottom is seven miles below the surface. So God sinks our sin under seven miles of seawater, and as Corrie ten Boom said, He places a sign there that says "No Fishing Allowed."

When God forgives our sin, He removes it as far from us as the east is from the west. God didn't say that He removes our sin as far as the north is from the south. If we head due north and travel far enough, we'll reach the North Pole. We can travel in only one direction from the North Pole—south! So, in that place, north meets south. But if you head due east, you can travel throughout eternity and never go west. East never meets west. So when God removes our sin as far as the east is from the west, we'll never see it again.

And here's the best part of forgiveness: God promises that when He forgives our sin, He'll remember it no more. God can't remember a sin He has forgiven. He chooses to remember our sins no more.

I believe that far too few people in the church understand this basic tenet. Far too many live without the assurance that a loving God has accepted them—a God who paid their penalty and offers the gift of eternal life to everyone who will believe.

When people receive the grace of God, when they choose a committed, intimate relationship with the God who gave His all for their reconciliation, that experience changes everything. They can have emotional healing, relational healing, and spiritual healing. Often, the power of this grace saves marriages.

God's grace makes it possible for you to forgive others and to restore relationships to a level of intimacy that can even surpass that which existed before. So, refuse to allow resentment to destroy your relationships. Discover the amazing power of God's grace to heal and to restore intimacy.

# Section Three
# Concern

# Concern and Tenderness

Legend has it that there was once an old stone monastery tucked away in the middle of a forest. Since the monastery was hidden in an out of the way location, people had to make a significant detour to find it. But find it they did. People came from all over to experience the peaceful spirit of the place. It had a healing influence on the soul.

As the years passed, however, fewer and fewer people made their way to the monastery. The monks had grown jealous and petty in their relationships with one another, and everyone who visited could feel the animosity.

Distressed by what was happening, the abbot of the monastery poured out his heart to his good friend Jeremiah, a wise old Jewish rabbi.

When Jeremiah heard the abbot's tale of woe, he asked if he could offer a suggestion. "Please do," responded the abbot. "Anything you can offer."

Jeremiah said that he had received a vision, an important vision, and the vision was this: the Messiah was among the ranks of the monks.

The abbot was flabbergasted. One among his own was the Messiah! Who could it be? He knew he wasn't the Messiah, but who was?

The abbot raced back to the monastery and shared his exciting news with his fellow monks. They grew silent as they looked into each other's faces. *Was this one the Messiah?* they wondered.

From that day on, the mood in the monastery changed. Joseph and Ivan started talking again, neither wanting to be guilty of slighting the Messiah. Pierre and Naibu left behind their frosty anger and sought each other's forgiveness. The monks began serving each other, looking out for opportunities to assist, seeking healing and forgiveness where offence had been given. And as the spirit of the monastery changed, the travelers returned. The word spread that the monastery was once again a place of peaceful repose.

What made the difference? When the monks thought the Messiah was among them, they began to demonstrate tender concern for each other.

We have been studying the book of Ruth as we search for components of lasting relationships. So far, we've found that commitment and character are major components of relationships that are fulfilling and enduring. Now we add one more component to that list. Partners in lasting relationships demonstrate genuine concern for each other.

In the book of Ruth, Naomi is the first one mentioned as demonstrating concern. She was concerned for her daughters-in-law.

> *Naomi said to her two daughters-in-law, "Go back, each of you, to your mother's home. May the LORD show kindness to you, as you have shown to your dead and to me. May the LORD grant that each of you will find rest in the home of another husband."*
> *Then she kissed them and they wept aloud (Ruth 1:8, 9).*

Naomi would have been better served if her daughters-in-law had accompanied her to Israel. They were her best hope of finding relief from her poverty. But Naomi's first concern was for their welfare. She believed that Orpah and Ruth would have a better chance of finding security in their father's house. They also stood a better chance of remarriage in Moab. So Naomi urged the girls to return to the place where their futures might be more secure.

Genuine concern places the needs of the other person ahead of your own. Genuine concern doesn't ask, What's in my best interest? Instead, it asks, What's in the best interest of the person I love?

When there's no mutual concern in a relationship, the chances are great that the relationship will fail. Ruth and Naomi exhibited genuine concern for each other. Naomi acted against her own best interests in imploring Ruth to return to her home, and Ruth demonstrated her concern for Naomi by volunteering to leave her home for an uncertain future in Israel—a land whose people and customs were strange to her. When Naomi tried to talk Ruth out of her decision, Ruth said,

> *"Don't urge me to leave you or to turn back from you. Where you go I will go, and where you stay I will stay. Your people will be my people and your God my God. Where you die I will die, and there I will be buried. May the* LORD *deal with me, be it ever so severely, if anything but death separates you and me"* (Ruth 1:16, 17).

Both women were willing to put the other person first. Both were willing to sacrifice for the sake of the other. Their concern for each other was obvious.

## Ruth's concern for Naomi

Ruth's concern for Naomi doesn't end here. When Naomi left Israel, she did so accompanied by her husband and her two sons. Her husband had come from a prominent family and may have been a man of some means. When Naomi returned, her station in life was quite different. Her husband and sons were dead, and she was destitute, with no visible means of support. No longer was she considered to be a leader in the community. Now everyone felt sorry for her. This must have been a bitter pill for Naomi to swallow; it was a major embarrassment in a small community.

To make matters even worse, in order to survive, Naomi would have follow the practice of the poor and glean behind the harvesters in order to have some meager portion to eat. She would now have to depend upon the generosity of strangers if she were to survive.

Ruth saw the sorrow and the shame Naomi experienced. She longed to spare Naomi the pain of becoming a public spectacle, so she volunteered to let Naomi remain at home while she gleaned.

> *Ruth the Moabitess said to Naomi, "Let me go to the fields and pick up the leftover grain behind anyone in whose eyes I find favor."*
>
> *Naomi said to her, "Go ahead, my daughter" (Ruth 2:2).*

Ruth was able to sense Naomi's pain and anticipate her need. And she was willing to make any sacrifice in order to meet that need; she was willing to spare Naomi the shame of gleaning. She would glean for the two of them.

Ruth and Naomi's mutual concern helped make their relationship something special. This shouldn't surprise us. Concern for others has always been at the heart of every great religion.

Judaism holds concern for others to be a basic tenet. In fact, an old Jewish legend speaks of two brothers who were wheat farmers. When the wheat harvest was complete, one of them said to himself, "My brother has seven children. I have none. With so many to feed, he could do with some help." So just before midnight, this man got up and carried a large measure of wheat to his brother's storage barn.

Meanwhile, the second brother was thinking to himself, "My brother is all alone tonight. I am so blessed to have a large family; I should do something to bless my brother." So, sometime after midnight, he got up and carried a large amount of wheat to his brother's storage barn. The next morning, the brothers were astonished to find their supply of wheat undiminished.

The brothers repeated their clandestine acts of generosity for several nights and still found that they had no less grain than when they began. Finally, on the sixth night, the brothers bumped into each other as each made his way to his brother's barn. When they realized what they had both attempted to do, they embraced. And, according to the legend, King Solomon decided to build the temple on the very spot where the two brothers met. He built the temple on the place of brotherhood.

Similarly, Christianity considers concern for others important. In fact, Jesus told us that His true followers would be easy to spot: They would be the ones who loved each other and showed their love through their actions. True followers of Jesus display concern for others.

Mutual concern makes relationships rich and fulfilling. Ruth and Naomi displayed a concern for each other that made their relationship sweet. However, these two women aren't the only ones in this story who demonstrate concern. Ruth went into the fields to glean so that she and Naomi would have something to eat. While she was there, Ruth caught the eye of Boaz, the owner of the field.

Boaz asked his field hands about Ruth. They were complimentary of Ruth's loving sacrifice for Naomi, and Boaz was impressed. Being a close relative of Naomi's now deceased husband, he knew Naomi well. He knew that she had fallen on hard times. So, Boaz spoke to Ruth. He said,

> *"My daughter, listen to me. Don't go and glean in another field and don't go away from here. Stay here with my servant girls. Watch the field where the men are harvesting, and follow along after the girls. I have told the men not to touch you. And whenever you are thirsty, go and get a drink from the water jars the men have filled"* (Ruth 2:8, 9).

Boaz didn't have to provide such courtesies for Ruth; allowing her to glean in his field was all the law required. But Boaz had a heart of sympathy for Naomi and Ruth. He decided to do more than what was required in order that he might provide for these women.

Why did he do this? Boaz answers our question in verse 11.

> *Boaz replied, "I've been told all about what you have done for your mother-in-law since the death of your husband—how you left your father and mother and your homeland and came to live with a*

*people you did not know before. May the LORD repay you for what you have done. May you be richly rewarded by the LORD, the God of Israel, under whose wings you have come to take refuge" (Ruth 2:11, 12).*

Boaz recognized in Ruth a quality that he wanted to display in his own life. He saw the concern Ruth had for her mother-in-law, and he felt compassion toward Ruth. So began a chain of concern. The chain began with Naomi's tender concern for her daughters-in-law. It continued with Ruth's loving care for Naomi. And it culminated in Boaz's kindness toward both Naomi and Ruth.

## Boaz's concern for Ruth

Boaz showed concern for Ruth by allowing her to glean in his field, to glean close to his workers, and to drink from the water he had provided for the workers. But he was just getting started.

> *At mealtime Boaz said to her, "Come over here. Have some bread and dip it in the wine vinegar."*
> *When she sat down with the harvesters, he offered her some roasted grain. She ate all she wanted and had some left over. As she got up to glean, Boaz gave orders to his men, "Even if she gathers among the sheaves, don't embarrass her. Rather, pull out some stalks for her from the bundles and leave them for her to pick up, and don't rebuke her" (Ruth 2:14–16).*

Boaz took such good care of Ruth that Naomi was shocked at how much grain Ruth had when she got home that night. She asked Ruth where she had worked that day, and Ruth said that she had gleaned in the field of Boaz.

Naomi was moved by Boaz's concern. She rejoiced in their good fortune and prayed a blessing on their benefactor.

> *"The LORD bless him!" Naomi said to her daughter-in-law. "He*

*has not stopped showing his kindness to the living and the dead"*
*(Ruth 2:20)*

As the days wore on, Boaz continued his kindness toward the women. Naomi began to realize that Boaz was taking quite an interest in Ruth. She saw an opportunity for Ruth to find a way out of her predicament, so she gave some womanly advice to her young daughter-in-law.

> *One day Naomi her mother-in-law said to her, "My daughter, should I not try to find a home for you, where you will be well pro-vided for?" (Ruth 3:1).*

Naomi wanted something better for her daughter-in-law. She wanted Ruth to marry someone who could provide for her, so she began to play matchmaker. Naomi told Ruth to go to the threshing floor where Boaz would sleep that night.

> *"Wash and perfume yourself, and put on your best clothes. Then go down to the threshing floor, but don't let him know you are there until he has finished eating and drinking. When he lies down, note the place where he is lying. Then go and uncover his feet and lie down. He will tell you what to do" (Ruth 3:3, 4).*

I love this part of the story. Naomi said, "Make yourself pretty. Use some of that perfume you've been saving. It's time you let Boaz know of your interest in him." Then she explained to Ruth, who was from Moab, what must have been a custom in Israel. Not much is known about this custom; this is the only place in Scripture where we find anything about it.

Naomi told Ruth to go to where the men were winnowing the grain. Once the grain was harvested, they had to separate it from the husks. They did this by having animals walk on the grain, thus breaking open the husks and allowing the grain to fall out. Then the entire mixture was thrown into the air so the wind could blow away the lighter, empty husks while the heavier grain fell back to the ground. Often, the winds were too strong during the day, so this work began around sunset. When the winnowing was finished for the evening, the work crew slept by the grain to protect it from thieves.

Naomi knew this, so she told Ruth to go to the threshing floor that evening. She was to hide herself and watch from the shadows until Boaz went to sleep. When he had fallen asleep, she was to uncover his feet and legs and then lie down at his feet. Eventually, the cold would awaken Boaz, and he would reach down to cover his legs. When he did, he would notice someone lying at his feet.

Why was Ruth to sleep at Boaz's feet? Lying at Boaz's feet would communicate subservience. Ruth presented herself as Boaz's servant.

Boaz was startled when he found Ruth at his feet. But Ruth was quick to let him know exactly what she wanted.

> *"Who are you?" he asked.*
> *"I am your servant Ruth," she said. "Spread the corner of your garment over me, since you are a kinsman-redeemer" (Ruth 3:9).*

Ruth said two things that made it abundantly clear to Boaz that she was interested in marriage. First, she requested that Boaz cover her with his garment. In that land, people would use garments in very symbolic ways. When a man spread his garment over a woman, he was symbolically claiming her as his wife.

Second, Ruth identified Boaz as "a kinsman-redeemer." Here Ruth was making a direct reference to the Hebrew law that required a man to marry the widow of a close relative in order to give birth to a male heir of the dead man's property. Ruth was asking Boaz to fulfill that function for her.

Boaz was touched by her interest in him. His response was just what Ruth and Naomi had hoped.

> *"The LORD bless you, my daughter," he replied. "This kindness is greater than that which you showed earlier: You have not run after*

*the younger men, whether rich or poor. And now, my daughter, don't be afraid. I will do for you all you ask. All my fellow townsmen know that you are a woman of noble character" (Ruth 3:10, 11).*

This was not a knee-jerk reaction to Ruth's request. Boaz had an interest in Ruth. He had been watching her carefully. In fact, Boaz had already considered fulfilling the duties of a kinsman-redeemer. We know that from his ready answer to Ruth's request.

## The kinsman-redeemer

In his answer, Boaz explained that there was another relative who was more closely related to Elimelech than he was. This other relative had first rights to marry Ruth. But Boaz said he would take care of it, and he sent Ruth home early the next morning with gifts—tokens of his pledge and esteem.

When Ruth told Naomi all that had happened that night, she predicted that Boaz would take care of the matter the very next day. She was right. Boaz made arrangements to marry Ruth, and when he did, Ruth didn't forget her mother-in-law. She brought her into her home to live with her and Boaz. When Ruth bore Boaz a son, Naomi helped raise the boy. Boaz and Ruth named their son Obed. He had a son whom he named Jesse, and Jesse became the father of David, the greatest king of Israel.

Naomi's tenderness toward Ruth had been reciprocated. When Boaz witnessed Ruth's concern for her mother-in-law, he showered both women with kindness. The circle of love continued as the three worked hard to out-give each other.

Although Ruth was somewhat younger than Boaz, they had the makings of a wonderful marriage. Their marriage was based on commitment, character, and concern.

If your relationships are to be lasting, concern must be exhibited in all of your interactions. Concern goes beyond identifying and meeting needs. It is even more than regarding the needs of others as more important than your own. While these are very important aspects of concern, it is also demonstrated by the words, tone of voice, and even body language you use in your daily conversation. Gentleness and respect must be evident in every communication.

People who wish to demonstrate concern toward their children won't scream at them, even when they are anxious to have them obey. Those who wish to show concern toward a spouse will never speak in a harsh tone or speak accusatively, or, on the other hand, clam up and refuse to talk. Genuine concern treats people with respect. It seeks to nurture and protect the beloved.

When I was a kid, at times I would speak harshly to my sister. However, when anyone else spoke to her that way, I was quick to defend her: "You don't talk that way to my sister!" As I grew up, I realized the hypocrisy of this practice. I should never speak to my sister, my parents, my children, or my wife in a way that I wouldn't allow anyone from outside the family to speak to them. Genuine concern dictates that I treat people with gentleness.

We all enjoy the company of people who are positive. They energize us, increasing our sense of happiness and acceptance, thus enhancing relationships. Research shows that something as simple as sharing good news can enhance marital satisfaction. Dr. Shelly Gable of UCLA helped author a research report that revealed how to increase a sense of satisfaction, intimacy, fun, and just good feelings about one's marriage. The study showed that when a person shares good news, if the spouse simply responds positively to the news, all of the aforementioned benefits occur. Dr. Gable said, "It isn't enough just to listen passively." Instead, she said, the partner needs to be active, offering hugs and even high fives. When the responder does this, the other person immediately has tender feelings toward the supporting partner.

Gentleness has a wonderful effect. It warms hearts, breaks down barriers, and invites a loving response in return. The world is hungry for gentle concern. Rebecca O'Connor discovered this while helping the victims of the Asian tsunami disaster. She said, "When I first saw the horrific images of the Asian tsunami disaster, I was working the night shift at New York Presbyterian hospital, where I am a pediatric nurse. I felt compelled to do something."

She flew to Sri Lanka, along with eight other medical professionals, for a two-week medical-relief trip. Arriving in Sri Lanka, they traveled through 150 miles of destruction before arriving in an urban area that had been completely devastated. They set up their clinic in a mosque and saw forty to one hundred patients every shift. Every day the team treated respiratory problems, foot and leg wounds resulting from debris hidden in floodwater, and a variety of other aliments.

After a few days, the medical team learned that they were less than a mile away from a hospital and another large clinic. O'Connor asked a Sri Lankan friend why people came to them when other options were close by. The friend said, "Because at the hospital, someone asks, 'Name? Age? Complaint?' and then gives them a sheet of paper and tells them to go wait somewhere. You sit them down, ask them what's wrong, and treat them. You listen to them."

O'Connor said, "It seemed that the most valuable therapy we were providing had nothing to do with antibiotics or wound care. By listening to story after heartbreaking story, admiring pictures of families once happy and healthy, and playing soccer with children who lost everything, we were able to say, 'We care about you, and we share in your grief,' without speaking a word."

When you warm the people you love with genuine concern, it changes the fabric of your relationship. Percy and Florence Arrowsmith discovered this to be true.

On June 1, 2005, Percy Arrowsmith, one hundred and five years old, and his one-hundred-year-old wife, Florence, celebrated their eightieth wedding anniversary. Guinness World Record authorities claim that the couple held the record for the longest marriage, as well as the greatest aggregate age of a married couple. Sadly, Percy died two weeks after that anniversary.

Percy and Florence met at their church in Hereford, England. He sang in the choir, and she was a Sunday School teacher. They claimed the key to their long marriage was that they wouldn't go to sleep on an argument. They said they always kissed each other and held hands each night before going to bed. Gentle concern was a hallmark of their lives together. The couple seemed to feed off the kindnesses through the years.

Naomi, Ruth, and Boaz understood the value of gentle concern in relationships. The more they showered each other with tender concern, the more they received in return. Why couldn't this be true of your relationships?

# Concern and Communication

A few years ago, I was shopping with my wife and daughters in a mall. After a couple hours of shopping, I sat outside a dress shop while the women in my life looked at dresses. As I waited, I began to engage in one of my favorite pastimes: people watching. I witnessed two very different relationships.

First, I saw a couple in their fifties. The man was dressed in business attire. His wife, who was very attractive, wore perfectly coordinated designer clothing. She wanted to buy a gift for someone and was anxious to get her husband's opinion, but he was obviously irritated by the ordeal.

The woman said, "Harry, I want you to see the sweater I'm thinking of getting for Martha. I want to know if you like it."

"Why does it matter whether or not I like it? You're going to buy whatever you think is best regardless of what I say," he snorted.

"I said that I wanted your opinion, didn't I? Why would I ask if I didn't care?"

"Whatever! You always say you want my opinion, but you don't really care what I think. You always buy exactly what you wanted to buy all along. You are the most self-centered woman I know," Harry replied.

The woman rolled her eyes and said, "Just once I'd love to get a civil word out of you. You never participate in anything having to do with the family. Don't you ever get tired of being so mean?"

Obviously angry, the man raised his voice, "Just shut up! Leave me alone and I'll be just fine! You get all worked up about this garbage because you don't have anything meaningful to do with your life. You are so shallow that you think finding the right color sweater is a life-and-death matter. Well, I don't give a rip what kind of sweater you buy. Just leave me alone!"

With that, the man stormed away, leaving an obviously wounded wife in his wake. It appeared that she choked back tears as she stood and watched for a while. Then she turned and headed off, I presume, to buy the sweater.

While I was still processing what I had just witnessed, another couple approached, probably in their late seventies. They were holding hands, and their body language told me that they enjoyed a relationship very different from that of the first couple I watched.

The woman looked at the man I presumed to be her husband and said, "Are you getting tired?"

"No," he replied. "I'm fine. Where would you like to look next?"

"Well, they might have what we want in Dillards, and if not there, perhaps Foleys will have it. But you were so sweet to come with me, I don't want to wear you out," she said.

He smiled at her and said, "I'm a pretty tough old goat. I'm just glad to be able to spend time with the best-looking woman in town."

The woman giggled and said something in reply, but by now they were out of earshot, so I couldn't hear the remainder of their conversation.

A more stark contrast could hardly be found than the one presented by those two couples. They both reminded me that one of the best predictors of the success or failure of a marriage is the quality of communication that exists between the spouses. People who display negative patterns of communication tend to have poor quality relationships; those who don't, on the other hand, generally demonstrate a higher level of satisfaction with the marriage and have a greater chance of success. When people communicate genuine concern, a successful relationship is almost certain to follow. I'm not talking about just the words that are spoken.

More importantly, I'm talking about the patterns of communication that exist in relationships.

## Examples of good communication

Examine the patterns of communication that exist in the book of Ruth. Notice first the tenderness with which Naomi addresses Ruth and Orpah after the deaths of Naomi's husband and two sons.

> *Then Naomi said to her two daughters-in-law, "Go back, each of you, to your mother's home. May the LORD show kindness to you, as you have shown to your dead and to me. May the LORD grant that each of you will find rest in the home of another husband"* (Ruth 1:8, 9).

Naomi exhibited tenderness and genuine concern for Ruth and Orpah. Naomi was concerned about their future and urged them to take a more secure course even though it would place her own future at greater risk.

Notice also how Ruth responded to Naomi.

> *But Ruth replied, "Don't urge me to leave you or to turn back from you. Where you go I will go, and where you stay I will stay. Your people will be my people and your God my God. Where you die I will die, and there I will be buried. May the LORD deal with me, be it ever so severely, if anything but death separates you and me"* (Ruth 1:16, 17).

While there is an unmistakable passion to Ruth's words, she spoke them with respect for Naomi and for her feelings. Ruth expresses an undying commitment to Naomi in some of the most beautiful language of love to be found anywhere.

We find another example of a healthy pattern of communication in the first meeting between Ruth and Boaz. Boaz saw Ruth gleaning in his field and inquired of one of his servants who that young woman might be. When the servant told him it was Naomi's daughter-in-law, Boaz showed great interest. He had heard of the tenderness Ruth had shown Naomi, and her character impressed him. So Boaz spoke to Ruth and told her to glean only in his fields.

> So Boaz said to Ruth, "My daughter, listen to me. Don't go and glean in another field and don't go away from here. Stay here with my servant girls. Watch the field where the men are harvesting, and follow along after the girls. I have told the men not to touch you. And whenever you are thirsty, go and get a drink from the water jars the men have filled."
>
> At this, she bowed down with her face to the ground. She exclaimed, "Why have I found such favor in your eyes that you notice me—a foreigner?"
>
> Boaz replied, "I've been told all about what you have done for your mother-in-law since the death of your husband—how you left your father and mother and your homeland and came to live with a people you did not know before. May the LORD repay you for what you have done. May you be richly rewarded by the LORD, the God of Israel, under whose wings you have come to take refuge."
>
> "May I continue to find favor in your eyes, my lord," she said. "You have given me comfort and have spoken kindly to your servant—though I do not have the standing of one of your servant girls" (Ruth 2:8–13).

Throughout the book of Ruth, the communication between Naomi, Ruth, and Boaz serves as a good model of successful communication. Their communication is characterized by positive tones and tender concern.

Genuine concern as evidenced through positive patterns of communication is a hallmark of lasting and fulfilling relationships. Conversely, messages communicating a lack of concern are characteristic of unsatisfying relationships. Negative patterns of communication, whether intentional or not, always suggest a lack of concern and practically guarantee relationship failure. In fact, a twenty-year study conducted by Scott Stanley, Howard Markman, and others from the University of Denver found that the existence of one or more negative patterns of communication in a marriage was the most accurate predictor of impending divorce as can be found. Further, their study demonstrated that removing one pattern of negative communication does more to ensure marital longevity than does adding five positive things to the marriage.

Communicating genuine concern for your spouse is essential in marriage. Removing negative communication is the first step toward communicating concern.

## Escalation

Stanley and Markman have named the first of these negative patterns of communication "escalation." This pattern occurs when a disagreement increases in volume and may even escalate into personal attacks, turning a small argument into a major event. Ted and Janet are an example of a couple who tend to escalate.

Ted and Janet came to me for marriage counseling. I asked them what they wanted me to help them with. The way they responded to my question told me what I needed to know. Janet started. She said, "We really need help with our finances—" But Ted interrupted. "That's not it. We need help with our sex life." Then Janet, obviously irritated with Ted's response, said, "Is that all you ever think about?" By now, Ted's temperature was skyrocketing, and he replied, "Well, someone has to think about it since it's obvious you never do! With you, it's all about money, money, money." To which Janet responded, "Maybe that's because you've never earned enough of it to make ends meet. If you were more of a go-getter, I might actually have time to think about something else."

At this point, I interrupted, "Wait a minute, guys! Look at what's happening right now. Your biggest problem may not be sex or money. It may be the way you communicate with each other. Does this pattern happen often with the two of you?"

Janet was first to speak. "All the time," she said. "We can't have a discussion without it erupting and growing to the point where we scream at each other."

Ted agreed. "I can't remember the last time we were actually able to talk about something without yelling. It drives me crazy."

I said, "Since you agree on this issue, let's address it first. Successful couples avoid this type of angry exchange. They know that when they talk to each other like this, the main message they're sending is a message that wounds. Successful couples recognize when this type of exchange is beginning, and they exit the negative cycle before they hurt each other."

Ted and Janet really did love each other, but both had so often wounded their partner by their words that the only message they could hear was negative. If Ted brought flowers home, the message of love was lost on Janet. She could hear only the hurtful words Ted shouted at her earlier that week. And the memory of Ted's angry words didn't leave Janet feeling very romantic, leaving Ted very frustrated.

Ted and Janet learned that mixed messages allow nothing but the negative to be heard. The undercurrent of poor communication drowns out any positive messages. When this couple learned to discuss a problem without wounding each other, they were free to feel the tenderness in each other's words.

## Invalidation

The story of Bill and Andrea supplies another example of negative communication patterns. Stanley and Markman call this communication pattern "invalidation." This pattern involves an attack on the person, character, feelings, or values of the other person. The attack may be intentional and openly confrontational or it may be more subtle and unintentional.

During a session in my office, Andrea brought up a concern about their marriage that she wanted to address. Bill made a mildly humorous statement about the issue, and Andrea immediately became very quiet.

When I noticed her silence, I asked, "What just happened here? Andrea brought up an issue she wanted to discuss, Bill made a joke, and Andrea quit talking. Andrea, why did you suddenly grow so quiet after Bill's joke?"

Andrea angrily blurted, "It's obvious, isn't it? He doesn't care! He doesn't take me or the relationship seriously. It's all one big joke to him."

I turned to her husband. "Bill," I said, "is that the message you intended to send to Andrea through your little joke?"

Bill, a bit surprised, said, "No—not at all! I was just trying to keep the whole thing on a more positive note."

Without realizing it, Bill had made Andrea feel unimportant. She felt he was making a direct attack on her and the issues she felt were important. Bill had made his wife feel as though she didn't matter. I don't believe Bill did this intentionally; he may truly have been interested in the issue and willing to discuss it. However, the message he unintentionally sent to his wife was that she was frivolous and silly.

Our motives may be pure, but that isn't sufficient. If we want to avoid doing harm to the relationship, we must be aware of how our spouse will interpret our message. This means that we must learn to communicate in a style that our spouse will understand, because men and women think and talk differently.

If one of my male friends comes to me and shares a problem, I may, after listening, offer a bit of advice. The typical male, if the advice seems sound, may feel that I have listened and been of real service to him.

However, if upon my return home, I find that my wife has the identical problem and I offer the identical advice, she may respond very differently than my male friend. In fact, she may ask, "Why don't you listen to me?"

I may well have listened to both of them and felt I was being helpful. But in treating my friend and my wife the same way, I have neglected to understand a basic difference between men and women. While there certainly are exceptions, in general, men seek solutions while women seek empathy. And women tend to bond through shared feelings, while men bond through shared activity.

These differences mean that I must respond differently to my friend and my wife even though the problem is the same. While it may be appropriate for me to offer advice about a solution to my friend, my wife would prefer that I empathize with her. What she wants to accomplish in sharing the problem with me is to feel closer to me when I gain an understanding of her feelings. When I empathize with her, she feels closer to me. To her, my giving advice seems insensitive and uncaring.

It is safe to say that most women will respond as my wife does. However, some women may be exceptions. The only safe course is for a husband to ask his wife how she would prefer him to respond in a similar situation. If he thinks he knows the answer without asking and is mistaken, his response will feel uncaring to his spouse.

Just as, like Andrea in my story above, a woman can misinterpret what a man says, so a man also can misinterpret what a woman says. A couple shared an example of this with me in a counseling session. After fifteen years of marriage, Juan and Christine have established the practice of keeping a weekly date night. They take turns planning the evening.

One night Juan planned to take Christine to a new restaurant he had eaten at during a business luncheon. He had really enjoyed the food and wanted to share the experience with her. That particular evening, this restaurant did not live up to expectations. Their waiter was slow getting to them, and when he finally took their order, he seemed distracted. Not only did he make mistakes on their order, but when the food actually arrived, it didn't live up to Juan's expectations. The entire experience was a disaster.

Christine commented on the sub-par service and the poor quality of the food, and immediately, Juan grew noticeably angry and withdrawn. Christine asked him what was wrong, but he didn't want to talk about it. In fact, he hardly said two words the rest of the evening.

In our session, Christine asked Juan why he had reacted as he had. He said that her criticism of the restaurant felt to him like a criticism of him and his ability to choose a good restaurant. Christine hadn't intended to criticize her husband, but to him it seemed like she was attacking his ability to plan a satisfying date with her.

Juan's reaction isn't unique; many men would react as he did. They may view criticism that isn't directed at them as an indictment of their ability to make good choices. As my wife says, "It's a male ego thing."

People in successful marriages learn how to navigate successfully the communication idiosyncrasies of their mate. They learn to communicate in a way that will ensure that their mate recognizes and receives their genuine concern.

## Negative interpretations

No one communicates perfectly all the time. At times, our best intentions are still misunderstood. At those times, we need a basic understanding of trust—which leads us to Stanley and Markman's third negative pattern of communication, "negative interpretations." A negative interpretation occurs when one party interprets what was said more negatively than his or her spouse intended. In one sense, the person who interprets things negatively is attempting to read the mate's mind. It is as though he or she says, "I know you are saying one thing, but I believe you actually mean something else."

Early in our marriage, Gayle did something that hurt my feelings. The incident was quite unintentional on her part, but at the time I didn't believe that to be true. I told her how hurt I was, and she apologized.

To Gayle, that was the end of the incident. I, on the other hand, didn't believe that she had been unaware that what she'd done had hurt me, and I wanted to make certain that she wouldn't do it again. Therefore, I brought up the incident again and told her how angry I was about it. Gayle listened intently and apologized again, promising never to do it again.

But I brought the incident up a third time. This time Gayle responded with just a touch or irritation and said, "You act as though I did this on purpose."

Convinced that she *had* done it on purpose, I responded, "Well, yeah. I do think so."

At this point, my young wife demonstrated a maturity that was well beyond her years. She took me by the hand, looked deep into my eyes, and said, "I want you to understand something. I will never intentionally hurt you."

That was a brand new thought to me. It was such a comforting thought that Gayle and I have made it the theme of our marriage. We will never intentionally hurt our partner.

Now be sure, there are times when I have inadvertently hurt Gayle— times, for instance, when I simply forgot that something might hurt her. However, I don't intentionally hurt her feelings. Gayle and I have been married for more than thirty years now, and I can truthfully say that in all that time, she has never intentionally hurt me.

Through the years, we've learned to trust each other on this point. Doing so frees me from trying to read something sinister into what she says or does. If I feel pain, I simply assume that the pain was inadvertent since she would never purposefully hurt me. I can then go to her and say, "I know you are unaware of this, but what you just said caused me pain." She always replies, "Oh, I'm sorry. Please forgive me. Help me understand how it caused you pain, and I will try to avoid doing it again."

This little agreement between the two of us prevents me from attempting to read her mind. I don't assume that she meant to harm me by something she says or does since she would never intentionally harm me. This has been a great blessing to our marriage.

## Avoidance and withdrawal

Finally, some couples fail to communicate genuine concern for each other by choosing never to discuss problems—a pattern Stanley and Markman call "avoidance and withdrawal." Some people find any discussion of a problem to be threatening, so they avoid it at all costs. They may change the subject or just not allow it to come up at all.

I can't tell you how many times someone has cried to me, "My spouse and I never talk. We never deal with our problems. We just stuff them and hope they'll go away, but they never do."

Avoiding a problem sends a frustrating message to a spouse. To the spouse who wants to deal with the issue, avoidance of it feels like rejection. You may be ignoring the problem in an attempt to avoid a fight with your spouse, but to your spouse, it feels as though you're avoiding him or her. This sends the message that you consider your spouse so unimportant that you don't even care to discuss problems with him or her.

Admittedly, many couples can't discuss a problem without allowing the discussion to deteriorate into a fight. They may need to see a counselor who can help them develop a problem-solving model. Once couples have agreed on a model for problem-solving, they find that they no longer need to avoid the problem since problem-discussion and problem-solving no longer result in fights.

Removing negative communication patterns from a marriage goes a long way toward helping couples communicate genuine caring for one another. When they remove negative patterns, they receive positive messages of love and concern without reservation. Since no one is sending mixed messages, the only message they receive is one of genuine concern. When you do this, your spouse will be able to say of you what Naomi said of Boaz: "He has not stopped showing his kindness."

# Concern and Her Needs

I met Roy and Ruby when I was working as a hospice chaplain. They had been married for sixty-seven years, but now Ruby was about to die of cancer.

Roy had fallen in love with Ruby when he was in high school. They dated throughout high school and college but didn't marry until Roy had completed an advanced degree and landed a good job as an engineer. They'd been almost constant companions, having never spent a night apart from each other since they were married. Their children couldn't remember ever having seen them fight.

The hospice nurse told the family that Ruby might pass away very soon. Ruby wasn't afraid of death, but she didn't want to be alone when it came. So, the family moved a hospital bed into Roy and Ruby's bedroom and made plans to take turns sitting with her until the end.

One night soon after, Roy couldn't sleep. He'd slept beside Ruby for sixty-seven years, and now the bed felt empty. So he got up and sent his son to bed. He would sit up with his sweet wife.

Roy turned the television on for a while, but after about forty-five minutes, he felt impressed to turn it off. He stood by Ruby's bed and reached down to hold her hand. Ruby opened her eyes to look at her husband, smiled, and then closed her eyes and died.

Roy, who was ninety-four years old, told me that grieving Ruby was the hardest thing he had ever done. It was obvious that the pain took its toll on him. I asked him if after all those years, he had any regrets. He thought a while and said, "I always thought we'd have more time together. I wish we'd had more time."

Amazing! After sixty-seven years of marriage, the last thirty of which they had spent in retirement, Roy's one regret was that he didn't have more time with Ruby! That's the kind of marriage I want. Don't you?

Roy showed tender concern for his wife. He cherished her. And that wonderful woman returned the favor, making Roy feel wonderfully loved. Every woman wants to be told that she is special to the man she loves—or, if not told that in so many words, at least to be made to feel that she is loved. Every woman longs to be cherished the way Roy cherished Ruby.

Men have a tendency to take women for granted. We have a tendency to fail to recognize just how important our wives are. Thomas Wheeler, chief executive officer (CEO) of the Massachusetts Mutual Life Insurance Company, and his wife were driving along an interstate highway when he noticed that their car was low on gas. Wheeler got off the highway at the next exit and soon found a rundown gas station with just one pump. He asked the lone attendant to fill the tank and check the oil and then went for a little walk around the station to stretch his legs.

As Wheeler was returning to the car, he noticed that the attendant and his wife were engaged in an animated conversation. The conversation stopped as he paid the attendant. But as he was getting back into the car, he saw the attendant wave and heard him say, "It was great talking to you."

As they drove out of the station, Wheeler asked his wife if she knew the man. She readily admitted she did. They'd gone to high school together and had dated steadily for about a year.

"Boy were you lucky that I came along," bragged Wheeler. "If you had married him, you'd be the wife of a gas-station attendant instead of the wife of a chief executive officer."

"My dear," replied his wife, "if I had married him, he'd be the chief executive officer and you'd be the gas station attendant."

## Boaz's tender concern

It is clear that Ruth and Boaz made each other feel very important. The night that Ruth uncovered Boaz's feet, making it known that she wanted to marry him, Boaz spoke to her with very tender words.

> *"The LORD bless you, my daughter," he replied. "This kindness is greater than that which you showed earlier: You have not run after the younger men, whether rich or poor. And now, my daughter, don't be afraid. I will do for you all you ask. All my fellow townsmen know that you are a woman of noble character" (Ruth 3:10, 11).*

Boaz demonstrated great respect for Ruth. He was complimentary of her. He also was anxious to take care of her and fulfill her requests. Boaz recognized Ruth's great value as a woman. He was anxious to demonstrate his tender concern for her. And she became his loving wife, bearing him a son. Boaz understood that women have some very basic needs, and he accepted the responsibility of meeting Ruth's most basic needs.

As a husband, it is my job to take the lead in our love relationship by meeting my wife's most basic needs. I'm responsible for creating an environment of love, acceptance, and praise where she will feel safe, loved, and enabled. If I meet those needs, my wife will flourish and grow. Her self-esteem comes primarily through her success or failure in family relationships. If she feels that she is a successful wife and mother, she is much more likely to be happy and feel good about herself. I have the power to help my wife develop a healthy self-image. I have the ability to help her feel good about herself by meeting her needs and therefore making her feel that I love her.

What are those needs? If you are at a loss to answer this question, don't feel alone. Sigmund Freud, the father of psychoanalysis, said, "Despite my thirty years of research into the feminine soul, I have not yet been able to answer the great question: What does a woman want?"

Well, Freud may not have been able to identify the deepest needs of women, but the author of the Bible has given us some important insights. Men, allow me to share three basic needs that your marriage should fulfill for your wife. Drs. Les and Leslie Parrott discuss these needs in greater detail in their book *Saving Your Marriage Before It Starts*.

## 1. Your wife needs to be cherished.

Your wife needs to know that she is number one in your life. She needs to know that if you had to choose between an evening with your buddies or with your wife, you would choose her—not because you had to but because you wanted to.

I have a friend who, in order to cherish his wife, gave up golf. He said, "Golf was eating up my entire day off. It was taking valuable time away from being with my wife, and she's more important to me than golf." He said that his decision was not right for everyone, but it was his attempt to cherish his wife. And it worked! Women spell *love* differently than men do. They spell *love* T-I-M-E.

What can you do to cherish your wife? How often do you say, "I love you"? In more than twenty-five years of counseling, I've had only one woman say to me that her husband told her too often that he loved her. Later, I learned that when this woman said that, she was having an affair and her husband's declaration of his love for her made her feel guilty. Most women are hungry to hear the words *I love you*.

But women don't want just to hear the words; they need to see them actually in action. Your wife will feel cherished if you take the time to call her during the day just to say, "You were on my mind." And have you ever sent flowers to your wife for no apparent reason? Make sure paramedics are handy the first time you do this; however, once she has recovered from the shock, she'll feel cherished.

I read about a couple who, for over half a century, played a special game together—a game no one else understood. The goal of their game was to write the word *SHMILY* in a place where the other would find it unexpectedly. Whenever Jim would find the word, it was his turn to leave it for Hazel to find, and vice versa.

Jim and Hazel wrote *SHMILY* with their fingers in the sugar and flour containers to await whoever was preparing the next meal. They smeared it in the dew on the windows overlooking the patio. They wrote it in the steam left on the mirror after a hot shower, where it would reappear bath after bath. At one point, Jim even unrolled an entire roll of toilet paper to leave *SHMILY* on the very last sheet.

Little notes bearing hurriedly scribbled *SHMILY*s appeared on dashboards and car seats or taped to steering wheels. They were stuffed inside shoes and left under pillows. *SHMILY* was written in the dust on the mantel and traced in the ashes of the fireplace. There was no end to the places *SHMILY* would pop up. This went on for more than fifty years. No one in the family understood the game or the meaning of *SHMILY*. Neither Jim nor Hazel would tell.

The day came, however, when Hazel died of breast cancer. Jim had stood by her side every step of the way. He had taken her to her treatments and slept by her bed when she was in the hospital. When Hazel died, Jim was holding her hand. And at the funeral, *SHMILY* was scrawled in yellow on the pink ribbons of one of Hazel's funeral bouquets.

After everyone had left the church but the family, Jim went to the side of Hazel's casket and began to sing to her. Shaking with sorrow, Jim sang, "S-H-M-I-L-Y—see how much I love you."

What do you think? Did Hazel feel that Jim cherished her?

As men, we probably have no idea of the effect we can have on our wives by being gentle and tender, making her feel cared for. Open the car door for her, hold her hand, rub her back, cuddle with her at times when doing so doesn't lead to the bedroom. Kiss your wife gently—often! Tell her that she is beautiful. Take time with the woman you married. Let her see how much you love her.

Does cherishing your wife mean that you will always sacrifice golf games, success at work, or nights out with the boys? Believe it or not, the answer is No. When your wife is satisfied in knowing that she takes first place in your life, when she knows she is the most important thing in the world to you, she will encourage you to do the things you enjoy. When a woman is truly, genuinely cherished, she feels free to encourage her husband's independence.

Gayle and I have a regular "date night." We protect our time together because we value each other so highly. However, one week we both had an appointment we couldn't reschedule that conflicted with our date. So we agreed that we would have our date during the day rather than that evening.

The day before our date, some friends came into my office and announced, "Mike, clear your schedule for tomorrow. We're taking you to a new, exclusive golf course tomorrow, and we're paying your greens fees."

I said, "Thanks, guys; it sounds great, but I have a very important appointment tomorrow."

They said, "What could possibly be that important? Break it!"

I said, "The appointment is with my wife. We're going on our date tomorrow, and we have a great day planned together."

My friends stood in stunned silence. They didn't know how to answer.

However, my wife was sitting in the next office, and she overheard our conversation. She emerged from her office and said, "Mike, you don't get to play golf very often. Why don't you play golf tomorrow? We can plan our date at another time."

Why did Gayle respond this way? She heard me make our relationship the priority. Since she knew that I cherished her, she wanted to make certain that I felt valued, so she sent me off to play golf. The important thing was that she knew I truly cherish her.

## 2. Your wife needs to be known.

Because your wife's need to be known is such an important need and because men and women differ so greatly regarding this aspect of communication, I'm going to repeat here some of what I said in the previous chapter. In fact, I'm going to expand on it a bit.

Has your wife ever said, "You're not listening to me"? In fact, at times you may be able to repeat most of what she's said for the past fifteen minutes, but she still insists that you haven't been listening. One night, in my office, a woman told her husband, "I've been pouring my heart out to you for the last twenty minutes, and all you've done is sit there and give me advice."

He said, "Yeah; so, what's wrong with that?"

"I don't need advice. I need to be understood!"

When your wife says, "I need to be understood," she doesn't mean that she wants you to understand the content of what she has said. She wants you to understand what she's been feeling.

Men, allow me give you a bit of advice: When your wife shares a problem with you, the last thing in the world you should ever do is to give her a bit of advice. Don't try to fix her problem. She doesn't want your solution—she wants your empathy.

For a woman, being understood means having her feelings validated and accepted. Men and women differ greatly in this regard. Dave Barry wrote, "What women want is to be loved, to be listened to, to be desired, to be respected, to be needed, to be trusted, and sometimes, just to be held. What men want is tickets for the World Series."

Watch how men talk to men and women talk to women. When women talk, they make eye contact and touch each other a lot. If a man reaches out to touch my hand when he's talking to me, I move away from him.

When a man shares a problem with his best friend, he usually condenses it to its most basic elements. Upon hearing the gist of the problem, the friend suggests a possible solution: "What you need to do is . . ." And if the solution makes sense, the other man replies, "Hey, thanks. You're OK!"

However, when a woman shares a problem with her best friend, the story takes considerably longer to tell. It seems to be important to include all the details—things such as what she was wearing that day and a full recounting of the conversation: "what I said" and "what she said" and "what I said back." At the conclusion of the story, her best girlfriend doesn't reply with a possible solution. Instead, with the hint of a tear in her eye, she says, "Bless your heart. You must have felt awful!" And upon hearing this reply, the woman says, "You're just the best friend I could ever have. You always understand."

Women listen intuitively and empathize, while men offer advice and lecture. When a man lectures or instructs his wife, she feels that he is treating her as though she is a child. No adult should ever be treated as a child!

One man said of his wife, "But at times she behaves so childishly!"

Even if that is true, her behavior should never determine your response. Men, you are responsible for treating your wife as an adult. She is responsible for her behavior. Your treatment of her is not dependent on your assessment of her behavior. Treat your wife as an adult and not as a child. Don't attempt to lecture her or instruct her. Speak to her as an adult—speak with respect.

Understand also that men and women use words differently. Men use words as a means of commerce in the workplace. Most of us do more talking in public than we do in private—up to three times more. Women, on the other hand, use words for intimate bonding. They say three times as many words in private as they do in public.

By the time a man gets home after a hard day's work, his words are all used up. His wife, on the other hand, has saved most of her words for him. A man can feel overwhelmed by the avalanche of words that greets him when he enters the house. A woman can feel that her husband's silence is icy when she's alone with him—that his silence says she isn't loved.

Men, if you want to meet your wife's need to be known, you must listen actively to her, reflecting back to her what she is saying and feeling, and genuinely wanting to understand her. But never, ever, ever should you offer a solution. Don't fix the problem; empathize with your wife.

Women need to have their feelings validated and accepted. They want you to see and experience the world the way they do instead of explaining to them why they shouldn't see it that way. If you can learn to offer a listening ear, an empathetic voice, and a comforting hug with a statement like, "You're hurting, aren't you?" or "You're under a lot of pressure, aren't you?" you can be married a lifetime! Your wife needs to be known.

## 3. Your wife needs to be respected.

When a man feels disrespected, he's most likely to react by becoming self-righteous and indignant. He may feel even more worthy of respect when women fail to act respectfully toward him. And he may show less respect to women until he feels he's getting what he deserves. However, women operate differently. When a woman isn't respected, she feels insecure and loses her sense of self.

A woman feels respected when her husband doesn't try to change or manipulate her but instead honors her needs, wishes, values, and rights. A woman feels respected when she is included in making decisions.

Once I bought a new car without consulting Gayle. She was not a happy camper. She hated that car. Part of the problem was that I bought a car with a standard transmission instead of an automatic. When I got it home, Gayle said, "I don't know how to drive a standard."

I said, "Oh, of course you do. Everyone knows how to drive a standard."

"I don't," she said.

"Well, I can teach you."

What a mistake! To this day, Gayle doesn't drive a standard.

A few months later, a tie rod broke while I was driving that car. It careened off the road and stopped in a field of dry grass. The catalytic converter caught the grass on fire and burned the car up. I got out just in time.

When I called Gayle to tell her the news, she asked, "Are you OK?"

"Yes, I'm fine," I said. "But the car is totaled!"

Gayle's response was, "Thank you, Lord!"—and I understood that she was as thankful to God for the demise of the car as she was for my safety!

Gayle wasn't unhappy with me simply because I bought a standard. I've owned standards since, and she's been just fine with them. She was unhappy because I made a big decision without consulting her.

I've seen men make career decisions and decisions regarding a relocation to another city without consulting their wife. Nothing will tear down a woman's sense of self faster than this. How can you have a happy marriage when she doesn't feel that you respect her?

Some men make fun of their wife in public. We've all seen men reduce a wife to tears by making jokes about her cooking, her housekeeping, her driving, or her looks. I've adopted a personal policy—I never make a joke at Gayle's expense, even if we are alone at home. If I hear a wonderful joke, I'll change it so that it's at my expense, never at Gayle's. This is my public policy, and it's my private policy. How can Gayle feel that I respect her if I'm constantly making jokes at her expense?

Respecting your wife also means supporting her in fulfilling her dreams and aspirations. I met a man who changed jobs and relocated his family to a different city so that his wife could pursue the career of her dreams. He could have complained about her career aspirations—after all, he had a professional life too. Instead, he respected his wife's dreams and helped her fulfill them. Some men feel threatened by the career success of their wife. It takes a man secure in himself to be able to rejoice in his wife's success.

Respect says, "I support you. I think you're valuable, and you don't have to be anyone other than who you are." When you meet your wife's need for respect, she'll be able to relax. She won't have a compulsive need to prove herself as an equal but will automatically feel and be equal. There is no better way to live with a woman! Your wife needs you to respect her.

Have you seen marriages like this? Have you seen marriages in which the woman's knight in shining armor is committed to meeting the needs of his fair princess? If so, have you noticed the glow on her face—the smile of contentment, the radiance that exists only in those who are greatly loved? If you're lucky, you see that when you look in the mirror.

Myrna has seen it in her mother's face. She wrote about it:

> My dad paints my mom's toenails. I was there when he started doing it. The whole family was at a resort to celebrate my folks' fortieth wedding anniversary. My mom has always been a beauty queen ever since she won a pageant when she was in high school. She really is pretty and has very nice hands and feet, too. She likes makeup and facials and perfume, and she always has had her fingernails and toenails painted. But when we were sitting out by the pool, I noticed for the first time that her toenails weren't done. I asked her why and she said she was getting too old and stiff to get down that far and she thought it was foolish to go to a beauty parlor to have it done.
>
> My father is a big, gruff man's man who has coached football all his life. I was really surprised when he spoke up and told my mom he would be glad to paint her toenails for her. When she asked him why he would want to do a thing like that, he said, "It's because I love you and want you to feel beautiful as long as you live."
>
> Five years later, he's still doing her toes for her.

Paul wrote, "Husbands, love your wives as Christ loved the church and gave himself for it" (Ephesians 5:25).

If you've never had a clue how to do that, now you're without excuse. Now you know that she needs to be cherished, known, and respected. You can do that. You can meet your wife's needs.

## Addendum to Chapter 8

Many people have found Les and Leslie Parrott's list of a woman's needs in marriage—the one discussed in chapter 8—to be of great value. Dr. Willard Harley offers a similar list. His book *His Needs, Her Needs: Building an Affair-Proof Marriage* has been of significant value to me and to many people I have counseled. As addendums to chapters 8 and 9, I'll briefly share Dr. Harley's list of the five most basic needs of men and women in marriage.

Harley has prioritized his list in order of importance, the first being the very most important need. If you are a woman, your list of needs may differ from Harley's, but that doesn't mean that your are in any way abnormal. Your needs are normal for you.

*1. What most women need most from their marriage is affection.* Affection is not sex, although it may at times lead to sex. Affection has to do with romance, tenderness, and touching. It takes the form of gentle touching, hugging, holding hands, or cuddling on the couch. It means remembering anniversaries, birthdays, and Valentine's Day with sentimental rather than practical gifts.

You show affection through moonlit walks and candlelight dinners. The saying of the words *I love you* or *You are beautiful* or *I love being with you* are forms of affection.

Most women crave affection as long as it isn't given to be manipulative. When the atmosphere of a relationship is affectionate, a woman finds it easy to respond.

*2. Women need conversation.* Women bond through shared emotions, and the most common means of sharing emotions is through conversation.

Most women are anxious to tell stories of their day. They can tell the stories with an amazing amount of detail while including a great deal of emotional content. This is an attempt to gain empathy rather than a desire for solutions. When a woman's husband empathizes with her, she feels close to her husband. She feels loved.

But conversation is never just one sided. In order to meet this important need, a man must be more than just a good listener. He must also share of himself with his wife. I encourage men to form the habit of finding one story from their day to share with their wife in some detail. If the man can associate an emotion to the story, all the better. This will help meet her need for conversation.

**3. *Women need honesty and openness.*** A woman needs her husband to be factually honest and emotionally transparent. Trust is essential if a woman is to experience intimacy. Where there is no trust, intimacy cannot exist.

This means that a man must never lie to his wife. He shouldn't lie to protect her, and he shouldn't lie to protect himself. He must adhere to a policy of complete honesty.

In addition, it is never wise to hide emotions from a spouse. Hiding emotions is not the same as controlling emotions. While emotions often need to be controlled, they must never be hidden. To hide an emotion is to be emotionally dishonest. Whenever one is dishonest, that person is violating trust.

**4. *Women need financial support.*** Fortunately, this doesn't mean that a man must become the next Bill Gates. It does, however, mean that he must keep a job and earn adequate income to meet the needs of his family. It also means that he must make sound financial decisions.

A woman feels her husband is providing financial support when she doesn't have to worry that the roof over her head is about to be taken away or that there will be no food on the table. There must be some security—however simple or even meager the lifestyle—for a woman's need in this area to be met.

It is perfectly permissible for a woman to hold a job outside of the home. This doesn't mean that the man has failed to provide financial security. If both parties agree, the woman may choose to have a career. However, it is usually best if, whenever possible, the couple budget on the man's income alone, leaving the woman's for extras. This gives her the freedom to quit work without sending her family into bankruptcy. While living on the husband's income alone isn't always possible, it remains a desirable goal.

When a man frequently loses his job, quits it, or is chronically under-employed, he runs the risk of failing to meet his wife's need for financial support.

**5. Women need family commitment.** This means that the word *divorce* cannot enter the vocabulary. Divorce is not an option. Solutions to problems will be sought, found, and employed.

Commitment may also be expressed in the amount of time a man spends with his wife and family. Some husbands will declare that they're giving "quality time" while they're not giving an adequate quantity of time to their family. Most women regard this as failure to be fully committed to the marriage.

Only one commitment in a man's life may supersede his commitment to his wife and children. That is a commitment to Christ. The man's commitment to his wife and children must supersede his commitment to his career, his parents, his siblings, and his friends. Again, most women will evaluate that commitment through the amount of time the man chooses to spend with his family.

Of course, no one will ever meet the needs of another human being 100 percent of the time. That is an unrealistic expectation. What women can expect is 100 percent effort and a willingness to learn. When that happens, she should count her needs as having been 100 percent met.

# Concern and His Needs

Nathan Birnbaum was a stand-up comic during the days of vaudeville. In 1923, when Nathan, whom everyone called Nattie, had finished his act in Union City, a friend of his brought her roommate backstage to meet Nattie. He took one look at this girl—barely five feet tall and weighing about a hundred pounds—and he knew he wanted to work with her. She agreed to join his act, and that's how George Burns and Gracie Allen began working together.

At first, Gracie played the part of the straight man with George playing the comic. But George noticed that Gracie got more laughs from her delivery of the straight line than he did from the punch line. So, George rewrote his material so he was the straight man and Gracie was the comic. "As a result," George said, "we were a great success."

Gracie's character had what George called "illogical logic." For example, Gracie would ask George, "Where do you keep your money?"

"In a bank," George would respond.

"What interest do you get?"

"Four percent."

"Ha! I get eight."

"You get eight?"

"Yep. I keep it in two banks."

George fell in love with Gracie but didn't tell her for fear that she might leave the act—she was planning to marry a successful vaudevillian named Benny Ryan. After almost a year, though, George told Gracie that he loved her, and eventually, she broke off her relationship with Benny and married George. When explaining how this took place, Gracie said, "I just want everyone to know one thing. I'm a very lucky woman. I was courted by the youngest, handsomest, most charming, most sought-after star in show business . . ."

"Thank you very much," George said.

"But I married George because I loved him."

America loved Gracie. She claimed to have grown grapefruits so big it took only eight to make a dozen. She confessed to cheating on her driver's test by copying from the car in front of her. And she claimed that her uncle Barnham Allen had the water drained from his swimming pool before diving in because he knew how to dive but didn't know how to swim.

Gracie had a heart attack in the 1950s and talked George into retiring the act in 1958. A few years later, she died. She and George had been constant companions for nearly forty years, and now he was alone. George wrote, "People often ask me how to make a marriage work. I know all about the importance of respect and trust and honesty and generosity. But for me the answer still comes back to one thing: marry Gracie."

Solomon, the wisest man who ever lived, said, "He who finds a wife finds a good thing, and obtains favor from the LORD" (Proverbs 18:22, NKJV). I must say my experience parallels that of Solomon. Gayle and I have been happily married for thirty-one years, and God has blessed me richly through marriage. I've found it to be a deeply satisfying experience largely because Gayle understands my needs as a man and has committed herself to meeting my needs—just as I have committed myself to meeting hers.

## What a wise woman does

Solomon, the author of the book of Proverbs, a part of the wisdom literature of the Old Testament, wrote of how a wise woman seeks to meet her husband's needs.

A wife of noble character who can find?
>   She is worth far more than rubies.
Her husband has full confidence in her
>   and lacks nothing of value.
She brings him good, not harm,
>   all the days of her life (Proverbs 31:10–12).

Solomon tells us that a good wife is worth her weight in gold. In part, her value is found in the fact that she does only good for her husband. Gayle and I have often said that one of the principles for a good marriage is the assumption that I mentioned in chapter 7: My mate would never intentionally harm me.

When you've made this assumption and then it appears that your mate has done or said something harmful to you, you may rest assured that a misunderstanding is involved. Either you have misunderstood what your mate actually said or did, or your mate didn't know that what he or she did would hurt you. Since your mate would never intentionally harm you, you may simply explain that what happened was in fact harmful to you, and your mate will make amends. He or she will apologize and make things right.

That is the picture painted in Proverbs. "She does him good and not harm for as long as she lives." This woman's husband is safe in making our basic assumption. The woman needs to be able to assume the same thing of her husband.

And you and your mate need to be able to make this same assumption in your marriage. The only way your mate can safely assume such is if you make sure that it is true. Never intentionally do anything to harm your mate.

Solomon tells us more about the value of a good wife in verse 23:

Her husband is known at the city meetings,
>   where he makes decisions as one of the leaders of the land (NCV).

Here, the husband of Solomon's ideal woman behaves as one who is respected in the city. He is a man of honor. And while he attends the city meetings, what does he do?

> Her children speak well of her.
>> Her husband also praises her, saying,
> "There are many fine women,
>> but you are better than all of them."
> Charm can fool you, and beauty can trick you,
>> but a woman who respects the Lord should be praised.
> Give her the reward she has earned;
>> she should be praised in public for what she has done (verses 28–31, NCV).

## Ruth and Boaz

Just as a good husband takes the lead in attempting to meet his wife's basic needs, so too should a wife respond to her husband's lead by meeting his most basic needs. When Boaz saw Ruth, he took the initiative to meet her needs. He saw to it that she could find plenty of grain when she gleaned behind his harvesters, telling his workers to leave extra behind for her to pick up. Boaz desired to provide for Ruth and to protect her.

> *Boaz said to Ruth, "My daughter, listen to me. Don't go and glean in another field and don't go away from here. Stay here with my servant girls. Watch the field where the men are harvesting, and follow along after the girls. I have told the men not to touch you. And whenever you are thirsty, go and get a drink from the water jars the men have filled" (Ruth 2:8, 9).*

Ruth learned of Boaz's reputation as a godly man from Naomi. She learned that Boaz could be trusted—that he was a man of pure motives. Every day as she gleaned in Boaz's field, he consistently demonstrated that he was trustworthy. This made her feel safe to respond to him in a very tender and intimate manner.

On Naomi's advice, Ruth let Boaz know that she was willing to respond to his kindness by returning the favor of met needs. After the harvest, she went to the threshing floor and waited for her opportunity.

> *When Boaz had finished eating and drinking and was in good spirits, he went over to lie down at the far end of the grain pile. Ruth approached quietly, uncovered his feet and lay down. In the middle of the night something startled the man, and he turned and discovered a woman lying at his feet.*
> *"Who are you?" he asked.*
> *"I am your servant Ruth," she said. "Spread the corner of your garment over me, since you are a kinsman-redeemer" (Ruth 3:7–9).*

The apostle Paul tells women to submit themselves to their husbands. A woman can do this safely only if her husband is trustworthy as a protector and provider. When a husband has demonstrated that he is trustworthy, his wife should respond in ways appropriate to meeting her husband's needs.

What are those needs? Again we turn to Les and Leslie Parrott's book *Saving Your Marriage Before It Starts* for the answers.

## 1. Your husband needs to be admired.

Your husband needs to know that you appreciate him and all that he does for you. Men derive their worth primarily from what they do. When a woman asks a man if he loves her, he'll often cite the things he does for her. "Of course I love you. Why do you think I work so hard at a job I don't really like so we'll have the money we need?"

While this is not always the primary way a woman wants to be told that she is loved, a wise woman will praise her husband for the things he does. It is important to thank him for the fact that he works hard to earn a living. Praise your husband for keeping the car in working order, for mowing the lawn, for doing the dishes, and for anything else he does to help keep the home running.

One woman told me that she refused to praise her husband. She didn't think her husband was very consistent in doing things to help around the house, and she feared that praising him would cause him to become complacent and fail to improve. She said that when someone withheld praise from her, she tended to work harder to prove that she was worthy of the praise she sought.

While the strategy of withholding praise in order to improve performance might have worked on that woman, when a man fails to receive admiration, he has a tendency to shut down and lose the motivation to try. He will begin to feel inadequate and incapable of pleasing his wife. He may stop trying altogether, and feelings of resentment toward his wife may build.

Some women make another mistake in this area. They nag their husbands in order to get them to perform at a higher level. Nagging tells a man that he isn't admired or respected. It also tends to cause men to lose the motivation to make a positive response. And again, resentment tends to build.

When a woman eliminates nagging and replaces it with appreciation and praise, her husband tends to respond more positively. Such an environment makes a man feel appreciated and loved, and he tends to become more like what his wife wants him to be.

Some years ago, a friend of mine decided to attend a meeting in a nearby city that I planned to attend too. This friend offered to give me a ride. On the morning of the meeting, he came to my house to pick me up. When I got in the car, I saw two women in the back seat. My friend introduced them as his wife and daughter and said they were going to shop while we attended the meeting. We exchanged greetings and headed out.

We hadn't been on the road very long before my friend's wife said, "You're driving too slow. Why don't you speed up?"

When he obliged, his wife said, "If you drive this fast, you'll get a ticket." So, my friend slowed down.

A little later she spoke up again. "Aren't you going to pass the car in front of you? He's going too slow."

When we pulled out to pass, we could see that a line of cars stretched out ahead of us, and my friend's wife said, "Are you going to pass all those cars?" Then, when he pulled back in line, she said, "We're never going to get there!"

As if this weren't bad enough, eventually the man's daughter joined in and started picking at her dad too. I was at first startled, then embarrassed, and eventually a bit angry with these two women.

We made it to our destination ahead of schedule and dropped the women off at a mall. I must admit to feeling no small amount of relief at their absence. Since we had some time before our meeting began, my friend and I went into a restaurant for a bite to eat. We just sat there, neither of us quite knowing what to say. Eventually, my friend asked, "Mike, what advice do you have for a man who has everything in life he could possibly want except for the one thing that is most important to him? What advice do you have for a man who doesn't have his wife's respect?"

Your husband needs to be admired.

## 2. Your husband needs to have autonomy.

Men need to have autonomy, and they particularly need it during times of stress. Women tend to respond to stress by reaching out to others and becoming more emotionally engaged. But a man responds to stress by becoming very focused. Those around him may think he's becoming withdrawn and disengaged, which explains why a woman sees her husband as being unloving or even mean during stressful times.

When a man comes home from work, he often finds a wife who is anxious to talk. He may still be thinking about the stresses of the day and therefore needs some quiet time alone. He views his wife's attempts to engage him in conversation as an invasion of privacy.

Here's how I encourage husbands and wives to approach this problem. First, I encourage the husband, during the drive home, to pick a spot a few blocks away from home where he can attempt to disengage from the problems of the day. I tell the couple that when the husband gets home, they are to greet each other with a passionate embrace and kiss. This helps them establish contact again, breaking down the walls created by their separation during the day. But then they are to refrain from conversation for the next fifteen to thirty minutes, during which time the man attempts to disengage totally from the problems of the day. When the "detoxification" time is complete, the couple should attempt to engage in conversation. This plan, or some variation of it, helps couples re-engage while preserving a man's need for autonomy.

After a hard day, most men need time to detoxify or regroup. They may do this by reading the newspaper, mowing the lawn, or playing a game on the computer. The objective is to provide them time to clear their minds before engaging in the relationship. A wise woman will give her husband the space he needs to regroup from times of stress.

## 3. Your husband needs shared activity.

While women tend to bond through shared emotions, men bond through doing things together. They bond through shared activity.

Perhaps you've heard of men who, while they enjoyed dating thoroughly, were dissatisfied with marriage. While the man was dating, his fiancée seemed to enjoy going to a ballgame or playing golf with him. But after the wedding, she lost all interest in such things. When this happens, a man feels cheated. He feels as though his wife lied to him to get him to marry her.

Men place a high value on shared activities. They play softball, golf, or tennis and go fishing or hunting together. When a man finds a woman who appears to enjoy doing these things with him, he feels that he may have found his soul mate. He feels closer to her when they do things together. When she no longer engages in these activities after the wedding, he feels she has distanced herself from him, and he begins to lose interest in her.

Women tend to bond by sharing stories of their day and the feelings associated with the stories. They touch frequently and show great empathy for one another. For the most part, men feel uncomfortable sharing with each other in this way, and rarely, if ever, touch while talking, unless they touch through a manly slap on the back.

My wife laughs at me for the way I communicate with my dad. When Dad comes over to talk, we usually go outside, because men often find it difficult to talk in front of women. We tend to lean against the car, both facing the same direction with arms folded. We seldom look at each other when we talk, and never once has my father said to me, "Son, how did that make you feel?" Gayle can't understand how men actually communicate in this manner. It all seems so strange to her.

Little boys long to do things with their fathers. They want to play catch or go fishing or hunting or engage in some other activity with Dad. This is how they feel connected to their father, and how they learn what it means to be a man. Men never outgrow this need for shared activity. It is a wise woman who understands this and makes the commitment to meet her husband's need for shared activity.

I am fortunate to be married to a woman who understands this need. She plays golf with me and overcame claustrophobia to become a certified scuba diver. I enjoy following professional sports. I follow the Dallas Cowboys, the Texas Rangers, the Dallas Mavericks, and the Dallas Stars. Gayle keeps informed regarding sports and keeps up with my favorite teams. I'm as happy watching a game with her as with anyone because she understands the game and enjoys it.

It wouldn't be fair, however, if we played only my games. I made a commitment to learning to enjoy and participate in some of her favorite activities as well. Therefore, I've now learned to enjoy parties, concerts, eating out as a form of recreation, and worst of all, shopping. After thirty years of marriage, Gayle says that I'm still learning how to be an effective shopping partner for her. Some skills come slowly!

Author and psychologist Willard Harley says that couples should spend approximately 80 percent of their recreational time together. There are times when "the guys" may appropriately do something together or for a woman to have a "ladies' night out." But a couple should spend most of their recreation time together. When husbands and wives commit to meeting the basic needs of their spouse, good things happen in the marriage. They create a marriage that can last a lifetime.

When I worked as a hospital chaplain, I was often called to the hospital in the middle of the night. On one such occasion, I went to the intensive care unit to comfort a woman named Velma and her daughter. The woman's husband, Jim, was about to pass away, and the nurses felt I could be of some assistance to the family.

I stood with Velma and her daughter and watched as Jim's life slowly ebbed away. Velma and Jim had been married for fifty-seven years. They met in Fort Worth, Texas, during the Depression. Velma was a nurse, and Jim, an elementary school teacher.

Velma told me how they had met. She had accepted an invitation from her eight-year-old nephew to attend his school's Christmas program, and Jim was her nephew's teacher. The two of them were attracted to each other immediately.

After the program, Jim asked if he could walk Velma to her apartment, and she said Yes. She told me, "On the way to my apartment we came to a little bridge that spanned a small creek. The moon was full and the night was beautiful, so we sat on the bridge dangling our legs over the creek as we talked and watched the moon. That's where it all began."

Velma spoke of Jim's gentleness. He had always been kind to her. His words were always tender and his attitude sweet. Jim had always made her feel very special.

Now, fifty-seven years and one daughter later, Velma watched as Jim breathed his last breath. We prayed and discussed a few necessary details. Then Velma's daughter said, "Mom, it's time to go."

But Velma didn't move. She stood by her husband's bed holding his hand.

"Mom, it really is getting late. We have quite an ordeal ahead of us. We both need our rest."

Velma smiled at her daughter but didn't move. After fifty-seven years, she couldn't let go of Jim's hand.

I suggested that the daughter go bring the car to the front of the hospital and said that I would bring her mother out to her. She agreed and disappeared through the door.

As Velma and I stood at Jim's side, I said, "It must be terribly difficult to leave him here."

"Yes," she said. "Maybe we should have fought more. Maybe it would have been easier then."

"I don't think so," I said. "Usually, when people have fought a lot, they have so many regrets that it complicates everything."

"Well, we certainly don't have any regrets," she said. Then she bent over, kissed Jim's forehead, and walked with me to her waiting daughter.

Fifty-seven years and no regrets! That doesn't happen by accident. It happens only when a couple employs all three components of lasting relationships. Only where commitment, character, and concern are combined do you ever find a relationship that can result in fifty-seven years with no regrets.

## Addendum to Chapter 9

As was the case in the previous chapter, I here offer an addendum to the Parrotts' list of needs. This is Dr. Willard Harley's list of the most basic needs of a man in marriage in order of importance. Dr. Harley's list comes from his research as well as from many years of counseling. However, men, you may find that your list of needs doesn't match his. This doesn't mean that you are in any way abnormal. It simply means that you are unique as a person. Make certain that your spouse understands your needs and how she can best meet them.

***1. What most men need most from their marriage is sexual fulfillment.*** It is very difficult for most women to recognize the strength of a man's sex drive. Men have an average of eight times as much testosterone as women. This may help explain why the male sex drive seems to be so much greater than that which most women have.

There are exceptions. Approximately 10 to 15 percent of men don't have a strong sex drive. This doesn't mean that they are in any way defective. Sex drive is usually a function of temperament or personality, and a man who has a low sex drive isn't any less of a man.

It is important that a wife be available to participate in the act of lovemaking on a regular basis. Most married couples in relatively good health between the ages of twenty and sixty make love two to three times weekly. This may vary according to age and health, as well as the age of the couple's children.

Women should take note of the fact that while a woman's husband should be the primary one to supply her needs, she can find partial fulfillment for some of her needs outside of marriage without violating the marriage contract. In certain situations and with appropriate people, she can legitimately meet a portion of her need for affection and conversation outside the marriage. However, were a man to try to meet any portion of his need for sexual fulfillment any place other than in marriage, that would be a serious violation of the marriage vows. This puts a man in a very vulnerable position in relationship to his wife. She is the only legitimate source for supplying his need for sexual fulfillment.

*2. Men need recreational companionship.* Every man needs to have fun with his wife. There is a little boy inside of every man. It is that little boy who makes him a comic or makes him love sports, hunting and fishing, or even video games. A wise woman will never attempt to kill the little boy in her man. Instead, she will learn to play with him.

Married couples should spend most of their recreation time together. Find activities you can participate in together, and make them a priority in your life. Establish a regular "date night" together, and plan fun activities. Make having fun a regular part of your marriage.

*3. Men need an attractive spouse.* This doesn't mean that women must become super models. That would be ridiculous! The media has imposed on us unrealistic, unhealthy pictures of feminine beauty. Women need not attain to such unrealistic standards.

But men are visually stimulated. Therefore, it is important that a woman try to keep her weight in line and learn to dress in an attractive fashion. Ask your husband what he enjoys seeing you in, and then wear that kind of clothing often.

Even what you wear to bed should be attractive. My wife has agreed to allow me to purchase her evening attire. If Gayle wears it to bed, I've bought it! I buy things I enjoy seeing her wear. Now, you must know that Gayle has a drawer full of mistakes. When she says, "Over my dead body!" I know I've goofed. Through the years, however, I've learned to choose things that she feels comfortable in and that I enjoy seeing her wear.

Do your hair in a manner that your husband finds attractive. If you wear makeup, do so in a way that he enjoys. Look attractive for him.

*4. Men need domestic support.* This doesn't mean that a woman should become a domestic slave! Her husband can and should help around the house. Most men, however, want their wife to be a homemaker. Decorating the house, cooking, cleaning, and raising children are important in fulfilling this need. The woman doesn't need to be solely responsible for any of these activities, but she will often be the primary provider of such things for her husband.

Gayle and I raised two daughters, and I was an active participant in that process. However, I must admit that Gayle did most of the work, and she deserves most of the credit for the fact that we raised two wonderful young women of whom we are both very proud. In so doing, Gayle fulfilled my need for domestic support.

**5. Men need admiration.** Ultimately, your husband will believe what you say about him. Further, he is likely to become what you say he actually is! If you tell him that he is the best father and the best husband you could have, he is much more likely to become all that you could want in a husband and father than he is if you constantly tell him about his shortcomings. Most men are more likely to improve in an atmosphere of acceptance and praise than they are to respond positively to nagging or criticism. The male ego is very fragile. It is a wise woman who treats it with care and nurtures it. If you desire to emasculate your husband, constant criticism and nagging will usually do the trick.

Again, it is important to know that no one will ever meet all the needs of his or her spouse perfectly. However, it is reasonable to expect that people who are committed to their marriage will make a good-faith effort to meet those needs. When they make such an effort, their spouse should consider that sufficient.

# Concern and Spirituality

Perhaps the most important lesson we can learn from the little book of Ruth can be found in something that is more implied than stated. If our relationships are to become everything God desires them to be, we must value genuine spirituality. Both parties must actively pursue a rich spiritual life, both individually and together.

Naomi, Ruth, and Boaz were all deeply spiritual people. This is very evident from their conversations. All three employ spiritual language. All three place a high value on spiritual principles and the will of God. In order for relationships to be truly valuable, this is an absolute necessity.

Many people misunderstand exactly what the term *spirituality* means. I've found it helpful to declare what spirituality is not before I attempt to define what it is. Spirituality is not church attendance, correct doctrine, healthy living, rule keeping, Bible study, reading spiritual books or magazines, prayer, or proper dress. While some of these things either may be used as tools to obtain spirituality or may eventually become expressions of spirituality, they are not spirituality itself.

So, what is spirituality? It is simply *seeking the face of God*. It is the desire to know God intimately.

Scripture assures us that we can seek and find God. The prophet Jeremiah pictures God as saying, " 'You will seek me and find me when you seek me with all your heart. I will be found by you,' declares the LORD" (Jeremiah 29:13, 14).

Knowing God differs from knowing about God. I'm a sports fan. I know a lot about my favorite athletes, but I don't know them personally. I've never met most of them and therefore can't say that I know them at all. Knowing batting averages or completion percentages doesn't give me intimate knowledge of the person. In order to have that kind of personal knowledge, I would need to actually meet the player, speak to the player, and spend some time with that player. Knowing *about* my favorite sports personalities is not the same as knowing *them.*

Knowing about God is not the same as knowing Him, and knowing God personally is the essence of spirituality. In order to know God, I must meet Him, spend time with Him, and know His mind.

Those who value spirituality will study the Bible for the purpose of knowing God, not for the purpose of just proving some doctrinal point. There is a time for doctrinal study, but not when pursuing genuine spirituality. The only question one should ask when studying the Bible for the purposes of spiritual growth is, What does this tell me about God?

While biblical knowledge may enhance our spirituality, it is not spirituality itself. I know people who know a great deal about the Bible but who don't know God. Their lives and conversation reveal that they don't know Him.

Meditation, prayer, and devotional Bible study are excellent tools for developing a personal relationship with God. Church attendance may also aid in this process. However, we can't use any of these things as measures of spirituality. The only measurements for spiritual growth are increased love for God and increased love for humankind. If you are experiencing an increase in these two loves, you can say that you are experiencing spiritual growth.

Spirituality is one of our most basic needs. We need to know God and love Him. The psalmist confesses to this need.

As the deer pants for streams of water,
    so my soul pants for you, O God.

My soul thirsts for God, for the living God.
When can I go and meet with God? (Psalm 42:1, 2).

In addition, we need to be meaningfully connected with others who know God personally. Such a connection will help nourish our relationship with God. It also is the secret for enhancing our relationships with other people. If a human relationship is to reach its full potential, both parties must share genuine spirituality. How can you expect to find real intimacy if you don't share intimacy in the most important area of your life?

This benefit of shared spirituality explains why studies reveal that Christians who pray together daily and share a corporate worship experience weekly enjoy much higher rates of satisfaction with their marriage and were less likely to experience divorce than were non-Christians. Couples who share a live, integrated Christian faith have better, more successful marriages. This is one of the reasons that pastors tend to discourage Christians from marrying anyone who is not a fully devoted follower of Jesus Christ. Scripture encourages us to follow this practice as well. Further, many pastors encourage their members to marry someone from within their own Christian denomination. They do this because they understand that the more things couples have in common, the better. You and your spouse will find it much easier to become spiritual soul mates if you share more areas of agreement than of disagreement.

A shared faith in Jesus enhances every aspect of marriage. Even secular researchers have discovered this to be true. From time to time, secular researchers ask the question, Who is having the most frequent and best quality sex in America? Invariably, their research reveals that Christians score far better in this arena than does any other group.

Not long ago, I was listening to a broadcast on public radio. The host was interviewing a secular researcher who had just completed an extensive study on sex in America. Again, this research project had sought to determine who was having the best sex in America. The researcher said that middle-aged Christian women in long-term marriages reported having the most frequent and best quality sex in America. The group that came in second was middle-aged Christian men in long-term marriages. This is not exactly the picture of quality sex presented in the popular media, is it?

When the host of the program asked why this was so, the researcher couldn't give a credible answer. She finally said, "I suppose there is a value to ritual."

Talk about being clueless! For all of her educational credentials, this researcher missed the point entirely. When Christ controls a life, He makes that person more selfless. Selflessness is a key component to having quality sex. When two people give to each other unselfishly, the result can't help but be satisfying.

The researcher missed something else. It has long been known that a very strong link exists between spirituality and sexuality. Highly spiritual people are also highly sexual people. This is one of the things about which I caution engaged couples who commit to praying and studying the Bible together. When a couple is in love and they add the spiritual component to their relationship, the attraction multiplies. Their hearts, minds, and bodies strongly desire a physical expression of their spiritual unity. Those who have made a commitment to sexual purity before marriage will actually find their commitment to be sorely tested because of their increased spirituality.

When a married couple makes a commitment to mutual spiritual growth, very good things happen in the marriage. Every aspect of married life is enhanced. Increased spiritual intimacy results in increased intimacy in other areas as well.

Since God designed marriage, why would we not expect this to be true? Do we actually believe that by ignoring spirituality we can improve on what God gave us? Do we really think that we can find a shortcut to intimacy?

God designed you as a spiritual being. Your spirituality affects every area of your life, especially your relationships. Finding a deeper relationship with God will improve your other relationships. Sharing genuine intimacy with your mate will take you as close to heaven as you can get while still on earth.

## For improved relationships through spirituality

I have a few suggestions for those who would like to improve their relationships through enhanced spirituality.

- Focus on your own personal, private growth in Christ through prayer, Scripture reading, meditation, praise, adoration, confession, and other spiritual practices. Make a study of spiritual formation through the practice of spiritual disciplines. Make certain that you know God intimately.
- Learn to pray together as a couple. Keep a shared prayer list. Learn to pray for the challenges your partner faces. Ask your partner to pray for you as well.
- Make the time to read the Bible together as a couple regularly. Discuss what you read. Apply Scripture in your daily lives. Together, ask these questions:

    What does this passage teach us about God?

    What does this passage tell us about how God feels about people?

    What do these verses tell us about how God would have us live today?

    Keep a journal of the thoughts you share as a couple.
- Share your walk. Tell your partner the story of your spiritual journey. Share your triumphs and your trials. Let your partner know about the things you are finding in your personal devotions.
- Commit to having a ministry together. Find an area of need in your church or in your neighborhood that you can meet as a team.
- Attend church together regularly. Worshiping with other believers provides a network of support and spiritual strength.
- Commit your relationship to God. Give Him full control over

every aspect of your life together. Ask God to glorify Himself through your relationship.

It has been my personal experience that these practices will change the quality of your marriage. As a counselor, I have seen couples achieve a level of fulfillment that they had never before dreamed possible.

As we have seen, there is much to learn about lasting relationships from Ruth. Commitment, character, and concern were characteristics that brought value to her relationships. They can do the same for you.

# Another Important Relationship

Sometimes what you don't find in a book is almost as intriguing as what you do find. I have the feeling that much good material was left out of the book of Ruth. There is much more that I want to know about this story.

For instance, I want to know something about the relationship between Elimelech and Naomi. Were they close? Had theirs been a true love story, or did they have to *learn* to love each other?

I also want to know something about Elimelech and Naomi as parents. How did they raise their family? Were they strict disciplinarians, or were they more relaxed? Did they have family worship, or was going to synagogue once a week and the temple once or twice a year the height of their spiritual life as a family?

Though much has been left out of the book of Ruth, the author of Ruth—as is the case with most good authors—seems to know that what is implied can be as powerful as that which is directly stated. So, while we have no direct information regarding my questions, we can make some basic assumptions. To me, the relationship Naomi had with Ruth and Orpah suggests that the entire family had been close. It would appear that Elimelech and Naomi loved and respected each other and their sons. When, after Elimelech's death, the sons married, the family simply embraced Ruth and Orpah with love. They included these two women as members of that close-knit family. Healthy families are characterized by inclusiveness.

We also find evidence of strong commitment in Elimelech's family. They were devoted to each other, and that devotion carried over into the relationship between Naomi and her daughters-in-law. So strong was Ruth's and Orpah's devotion to Naomi that when their husbands died and Naomi learned that the famine in Israel was over, the girls just assumed that they would accompany Naomi as she returned to Israel.

> *Now Elimelech, Naomi's husband, died, and she was left with her two sons. They married Moabite women, one named Orpah and the other Ruth. After they had lived there about ten years, both Mahlon and Kilion also died, and Naomi was left without her two sons and her husband.*
>
> *When she heard in Moab that the LORD had come to the aid of his people by providing food for them, Naomi and her daughters-in-law prepared to return home from there. With her two daughters-in-law, she left the place where she had been living and set out on the road that would take them back to the land of Judah. (Ruth 1:3–7).*

If our assumptions are correct, we might wonder how Elimelech and Naomi pulled it off. How did they raise boys who were healthy, happy, and committed to their parents? How did they raise boys who would commit themselves to a spouse? Most parents would love to know the secret of raising happy children who possess good values. In fact, a study titled "A Lot Easier Said Than Done" revealed that the greatest source of worry for parents today is raising children who are well behaved and have good values. Parents viewed their biggest challenges as protecting children from negative influences and finding family time.

This study found that parents feel overwhelmed by the challenges of raising children. Seventy-six percent of parents with children between ages five and seventeen said they believe it is "a lot harder" to raise children today than when they were growing up. Sixty-one percent thought they were doing a bad job. They gave themselves bad marks on their own parenting.

My children are grown now, but I must admit that parenting was the single most guilt-producing activity of my entire life. I never felt I had done enough, and I never felt that I really was a good parent. In spite of that, our daughters are happy, well-balanced adults who seem to feel no need for therapy to recover from my bad parenting. They both reassure me that I did a good job as their father. At the time, however, I felt very guilty about the job I was doing.

The Bible shares some simple principles for parenting that helped guide me as I partnered with my wife to raise our children. One of these principles is found in Proverbs: "Train a child in the way he should go, / and when he is old he will not turn from it" (Proverbs 22:6). The wise man suggested affirmative, purposeful action. It suggests that parents should identify values they want to instill in their children and then set about to instill them.

## Fearful of being parents

I find that many people who are raising children today are afraid to be parents. In fact, it appears to me that many adults are afraid of their children. They're afraid to say No to them. Not long ago, I was in a restaurant where I saw this played out between a woman and her five-year-old daughter.

The woman wanted her daughter to make a healthy choice of food, but her daughter wanted ice cream. The mother pleaded with her daughter, but the daughter was resolute. When the mother suggested that the daughter might need to eat something healthy first, the daughter pitched a fit. She screamed and cried until her mother gave in and ordered ice cream!

As they ate, the daughter decided that she was bored, so she got out of her chair and began to visit people at nearby tables. The mother pled with her daughter to return to her seat and finish her ice cream, but the daughter ignored the pleas. She continued to do exactly as she wanted, almost defying her mother to act.

Then Mom changed tactics and spoke in a harsh voice, but the little princess continued to ignore her mother. She knew her mother was too frightened to actually do anything.

The girl became quite a nuisance to the other patrons in the restaurant, and customers began to give the mother dirty looks because of her failure to control her child. In desperation, the mother said, "If you don't come back here, you can't watch television tonight."

At that, the girl looked at her mother and said, "I'm not going to let *you* watch television, Mommy!"

Mom looked at the other customers and shrugged her shoulders as though she had done everything possible—the situation was simply hopeless.

This woman was afraid to be the parent. Her daughter had intimidated her. The woman wasn't willing to set boundaries for her daughter or to enforce consequences when the boundaries were crossed. If you would produce healthy adults out of your children, you must be the parent.

What does that mean?

Being the parent means that you communicate love to your children. Children must first know that their parents love them and accept them. Then, out of that relationship of love, you must establish definite boundaries and you must announce and enforce consequences for violating those boundaries.

Boundaries are simply rules for living. These rules should be few, but they should be consistently enforced. Failure to enforce a rule is worse than not having any rules at all because it teaches children to disrespect the rules. The best consequences are natural consequences, but whatever the consequence is, you must enforce it *every time the rule is broken*. At first, this takes a lot of energy, but if you begin early in a child's life and you are persistent, you should have fewer problems later in the child's life.

Children must learn to mind their parents. You do your children no favor if you fail to make them mind. Children who respect their parents are happier than those who don't. As always, this respect must come from a relationship of love. Rules without love produce angry, rebellious children. Love without rules produces undisciplined children. To obtain the best outcome, you must combine love and rules.

As our children grew older, Gayle and I negotiated rules and consequences with them. They could aid in establishing the rules for living and the consequences for breaking the rules. Gayle and I always had veto power, but we seldom had to use it.

Once a rule was established and a consequence decided upon, when it was broken, I would say, "I respect you and your power of choice so much that I would never withhold from you a consequence you have freely chosen." Then I would administer the consequence. This removed the focus from Gayle and me and from the punishment and placed it on the choices our children made. They learned that they could control their happiness by making good choices.

Being the parent means establishing rules from a relationship of love and then consistently enforcing those rules. This teaches children to respect you and to respect themselves.

## Passing along your values

Being the parent also means deciding which values to teach your children. I've heard some parents say that they weren't going to "force" a set of values or a brand of religion on their children. Instead, they were going to wait until their children were older and then allow them to choose for themselves. This always results in confused adults who have few values and no religion. Parents must choose the values and religion and then teach them to their children.

Once parents have decided on the values, they plan how they're going to teach those values and then they put the plan into action. Teaching is done verbally at times. Reading or telling stories from Scripture is an excellent way to teach values to children. The Bible is filled with wonderful stories that will teach life lessons more effectively than any other method.

Occasionally, as our children were growing, Gayle and I would witness a real-life demonstration of values or the lack of them. For instance, we might see a child speak in a disrespectful manner toward a parent. Whenever we saw such things, we would talk with our children about what they had just witnessed. We might say something like, "You know, in our family, we do things differently. We have chosen to speak with love and respect to Mommy and Daddy." We stated the value as an established fact that served as an identifying characteristic of our family. Our children became proud of the fact that our family did things in a certain way. And they began to see the wisdom of such choices.

Dad, if you want your children to learn to value their mother, you must speak well of her and require that your children do so too. If you want your children to know and love God, you must teach them of your love for God. You must read the Bible stories to them and share your insights regarding the stories.

We also teach through example. Studies show that children are far more likely to attend church as adults if Mom and Dad both attend church with their children every week. If neither Mom nor Dad attend church, children are most unlikely to attend. Children are a little more likely to attend church if only Mom attends, and even more likely to attend if only Dad attends. But children are most likely to attend church if Mom and Dad attend together with the family on a weekly basis. Our example teaches children well, so we must instill our values in our children through word and example. We shouldn't be afraid to act in positive, assertive ways to infuse our children with positive values.

Moms and dads are to teach their children. They are to decide on the values their children should learn and then be intentional about teaching those values. The author of Proverbs speaks of this:

My son, keep your father's commands
    and do not forsake your mother's teaching.
Bind them upon your heart forever;

fasten them around your neck.
When you walk, they will guide you;
>    when you sleep, they will watch over you;
>    when you awake, they will speak to you.
For these commands are a lamp,
>    this teaching is a light,
and the corrections of discipline
>    are the way to life (Proverbs 6:20–23).

## Fathers' important role

One of the components of my ministry has been to serve as a counselor. I've received training and hold a master's degree in this area. However, my training didn't prepare me for the type of counseling I find myself doing now. As I counsel people in their twenties, thirties, and, at times, even in their forties, I find that what I'm actually doing is parenting! I'm parenting people who weren't parented well. I teach values that parents should have taken time to instill in my counselees when they were very young.

Fathers are particularly absent from the parenting scene today. Many of them have abdicated their role, whether because of a divorce or simply because of inattention to their children. This is having a devastating effect on children—an effect that lasts well into adulthood.

It is from her father that a girl learns that she is to be cherished. It is from her father that a girl learns who she is in the world, especially in regard to men. A girl should learn from her father that she is pretty, talented, strong, competent, and deserving of respect and protection. It is through the relationship with her father that a girl learns how to converse with men.

Girls who don't enjoy a relationship of tenderness with their fathers develop what some call "father hunger." Women may spend their entire life looking for what they missed. Often, they're willing to give themselves away for any bit of attention from a man. In a subconscious attempt to resolve issues they still have regarding their father, many women marry men who remind them of him.

My wife's father, Jack, raised two sons and three daughters. He would read to them at night. They would all pile on his bed and lay their heads on his arms as he shared his love of good literature with his tribe. He had pet names for each child and treated all of them with great tenderness and respect. He understood his daughters' needs. He taught them, as well as his sons, to work with their hands in his glass shop.

Jack's children knew that he was always on their side, always believed in them, and was always proud of them. The girls knew they were pretty, and they loved it when their daddy bought them new dresses.

My wife, Gayle, has always found it easy to be close to me. She knows who she is in the world and understands how she relates to men. I give much of the credit for this to my father-in-law. He was a man who understood what it means to be a father. His tenderness with his daughters has paid dividends to me through the years of my marriage. I have him to thank for that.

Fathers have great influence on their sons as well. Some lessons a boy can learn only from Dad. Fathers must teach life skills, self-esteem, and spiritual priorities to their sons. Sons learn from fathers how men treat women and children. Boys learn that they are capable from a father's approval. In short, a boy learns how to be a man from his father.

John Eldridge writes that manhood is not something that someone acquires simply by turning twenty-one years of age. Someone must bequeath manhood to a boy. Someone must tell a boy that he measures up—that he is of value. Someone must tell a boy that he is a man. That someone must be the boy's father.

Again, allow me to use my father-in-law as an example. As his boys were growing up, Jack taught them how to behave themselves. He insisted that they eat dinner together as a family, and there he taught his boys manners.

Jack also used dinnertime as an opportunity to become a living demonstration of manhood and to elevate his wife in the eyes of his children. He would compliment her at the dinner table in front of them. He would tell his children how lucky they were to have a mother like her. As a result, his sons always held their mother in the highest esteem and always treated their girlfriends with respect.

It seems that today, some boys never grow up. I know young men in their twenties, thirties, and even forties who haven't grown up. They have what psychologists call the "Peter Pan syndrome." You remember Peter Pan; he was the boy who declared, "I'll never grow up!" Unless a boy sees the value of becoming a grown up, a value he sees in his father, he has great difficulty ever assuming the role of a man.

A father's words have the power to elevate and heal, and they have the power to belittle and kill. Fathers who are critical of their sons are telling them that they don't measure up, aren't good enough, and will never be men. Fathers who tell sons that they are of value, are competent, strong, capable, and innately spiritual persons, are giving their sons the gift of manhood.

As a pastor and counselor, I can tell you that there is a terrible dearth of true men today. Too few are willing to be men and truly father their children. Too few understand what manhood really is and what it is not. Too few men are willing to stand up and be counted. As one author puts it, "The greatest want of the world is the want of men."

While we have no direct evidence to support this, I believe that Elimelech was a man who understood manhood and bequeathed manhood to his boys. The evidence is indirect, but for me it is convincing. When I look at Naomi, I see a woman who was made strong not just by a father but also by a loving husband. I see sons made strong by a father. They were made so strong that they chose to marry women who were also strong—strong enough to love Naomi and become devoted to her even after the deaths of their husbands. I believe Elimelech was a good husband and father.

## The power of mothers

The evidence for the quality of Naomi's work as a mother is much more direct. We see her interaction with her daughters-in-law and find it to be very positive. Naomi reminds us of the tremendous influence mothers have on the life of their children. One author has referred to motherhood as the highest calling on earth. The Bible is full of wonderful examples of motherhood. We think of Hannah and her son Samuel, or Jochebed with Moses. These women had a wonderful influence on their children, and the world is richer because of it.

Mothers have the power to change the world. As mothers patiently, lovingly train their children, life lessons are learned and characters are formed. Mothers teach their daughters life skills such as how to make piecrust and gravy, how to put in a zipper, and how to keep house. Mothers teach daughters how to do their hair, engage in society, shop, relate to a husband, and handle a career. It is in her that a girl finds an example of sexuality, appropriateness, loyalty, service, and the role of women. She learns how to raise her children, relate to a spouse, and obey God, all from her mother. In short, a girl learns to be a woman by watching her mother.

I can remember my wife saying something to our daughters and then, in a moment of privacy, telling me, "I have become my mother! I hear her words coming out of my mouth." Fortunately, this was not a bad thing!

When a mother is dysfunctional, manipulative, nagging, critical, or angry, tremendous harm is done. When a mother is absent, never finding time for her children, she sends a message that her children are unimportant or a bother.

As a counselor, I have spent many hours listening to the tearful tales of women as they describe their pain over a negative relationship with mothers. By contrast, I don't get many women in my counseling office who've had a positive relationship with mom. Life tends to turn out better for such fortunate women.

Mothers also have a great influence over their sons. The knowledge that their mother is praying for them has changed the life of many men.

I remember a story of a young man who was serving in Europe during World War II. During one particularly fierce battle, a sergeant ordered this young private to run across a stretch of open field to carry a message to another squad. Bullets filled the air, making it likely that the young man would be hit.

When the private received the order, he looked at his watch and hesitated.

The sergeant yelled, "Soldier, didn't you hear my order?"

The young man looked at his watch again and still hesitated.

The sergeant yelled once more, and again the young man looked at his watch without making a move to go.

Finally, the sergeant screamed, "What are you waiting for, soldier?"

The private answered, "My mother prays for me every day at five P.M. It will be five P.M. back home in just another thirty seconds. I'm waiting to make my run until I know my mother is praying for me."

Mothers serve as a source of encouragement for their boys. No one else sees the man inside them as their mothers can.

Mothers help their sons have a positive sexual identity. An overbearing mother can confuse her son in this area. A tender, encouraging mother can help her son see himself as the man God intended him to be.

A father may teach strength and justice to his son, but a mother teaches tenderness, empathy, and pity. Often, mothers are the parent who most frequently has worship with the children. This makes them very important in a son's spiritual development. I know my mother had a great influence on my spiritual development. That godly woman greatly affected my relationship with God.

Mothers typically do the lion's share of work in raising their children. They often spend more time with their children than the fathers do. This makes their work all the more important.

I believe Naomi was a woman who took motherhood seriously. Her relationship with her daughters-in-law would suggest that this is true. When Ruth married and had a son, she brought Naomi into her home, and Naomi assisted Ruth in raising Obed. He became the father of Jesse, who became the father of David—the greatest king in Israel's history. So, Naomi's commitment to being the best wife, mother, mother-in-law, and grandmother possible paid dividends for generations! Never underestimate the value of your commitment to parenting your children.

If you are looking forward to becoming a parent, I urge you to commit yourself prayerfully to your children even before they are born. Ask

God to give you positive parental examples. Learn rich lessons from your own childhood, and glean from those memories that which is best.

Perhaps you are currently parenting children in your home. It isn't too late to become a better parent. Spend time on your knees asking for wisdom, patience, and greater love for your children.

If your children are adults and have left your home, don't forget that you are still a parent. You still have a work to do in parenting your adult children. That work now takes the form of a godly example rather than hands-on parenting.

If your children are grown, you may now have the exciting job of serving as a grandparent. I know several couples who tell me that they are doing a much better job as grandparents than they ever did as parents. As such, they are having a positive effect on the lives of children—an effect that will last for years to come.

There is much that we don't know about Elimelech and Naomi. Much has not been told. However, we can see evidences of genuine commitment. The kind of legacy they left is usually built upon a strong commitment to marriage and family. Elimelech and Naomi are people who, I believe, made their marriage and their children a priority. Their efforts paid off—King David, the man after God's own heart, may be our best proof of this. With God's blessing, your efforts will too!

**When the Parenting You Received Was Destructive . . .**

Some who are reading this book are wondering what they can do to deal with the very negative parenting they received as children. Here are a few suggestions.

**1. Recognize that your parents have passed along a legacy that has affected you.** Some things will be good and other things will not. Don't ignore the good that comes from even the worst of homes. By the same token, don't ignore the negative or even destructive things that have come from your past. You'll never effectively deal with anything that you ignore. Healing comes only as you confront the past and reconcile yourself to it.

**2. Examine your behavior to find the positive and the negative patterns you have learned from your family.** Be careful to identify the positives and be open to embracing them. Be brutally honest about the negative. Don't gloss over things that may be painful to deal with.

**3. Realize that the cycle of negative patterns must be broken before you can parent your own children effectively.** You may begin this by making a journey of forgiveness for the failures of your own parents. Harbored resentment will prevent you from ever growing personally. Your tendency will always be to repeat the failures of your parents. It is extremely difficult to change negative behavior without first forgiving those who helped create the behavior in the first place.

**4. Ask God to heal you.** Ask God to give you a new identity. John the Revelator tells us that God will give the redeemed a new name. That means that God will give us a new identity, new behaviors, and new attitudes. He alone can do this. Your new name won't be the one you've had in this world. It will be a name that God gives you. Your new name will be representative of your new life patterns.

**5. Trust that God, your heavenly Parent, has called you to be a parent.** Trust that He can heal your childhood wounds. Understand that His opinion of you overrides that of any earthly parent and overcomes any of their mistakes. Your heavenly Father can heal the wounds inflicted by even the most severe childhood abuse. He can make you new. As a young woman who was recovering from childhood abuse told me, "It's never too late to have a happy childhood!"

**6. Commit yourself to a journey of parenting with God at your side.** Claim His promise that He will be with you always. Ask that He parent your children through you. God wants you to have a positive influence for generations to come. He longs for you to be a parent who makes a difference. Best of all, He will make it possible for you to succeed in this most important work.

# Final Thoughts

Monroe and Bonnie had been married for more than fifty years. When I met Bonnie, she was a patient of the hospice where I served as chaplain. She had only a few more weeks to live.

Bonnie was a woman of few words. When I visited, I would attempt to engage her in conversation, hoping that she would open up about her impending death. Bonnie, however, was very adept at answering my open-ended questions with a simple Yes or No. She just wasn't interested in talking.

One day I brought my Bible and read a chapter from one of the Gospels. I shared some commentary as we went through the chapter, and then I closed with prayer.

After my prayer, Bonnie said, "Now that's what I like!" Needless to say, I brought my Bible with me for every visit from then on.

The nurses were concerned about Bonnie's husband, Monroe. He was a Texan from the old school who spoke with a heavy drawl in a deep, bass voice. He, too, was a person of few words, and he never spoke openly in front of women. Whenever I visited, Monroe and I would step out onto the back porch, out of earshot of the women, and have our chats together.

Chatting with Monroe took some patience and no small amount of skill. Like his wife, Monroe tended to answer all questions with a simple

Yep or Nope. It was difficult for him to open up and share his thoughts and emotions.

When I observed Monroe and Bonnie together, I saw that they spoke very little. They were matter of fact and preferred single syllable responses. Their children confirmed that they just didn't talk very much. No one doubted that they loved each other, but you couldn't tell it by how they talked.

One day I was called to Bonnie's bedside because the nurses felt she would soon die. I asked Bonnie about her salvation, and she assured me that things were just fine between her and God. So I prayed for her.

During my prayer, Monroe and Bonnie's sister stepped into the room. When I looked up after my prayer, I saw Monroe looking at Bonnie, and I said, "Bonnie! Do you see that? Do you see the look in Monroe's eyes?"

Startled, Bonnie stared intently at her husband's eyes—eyes that were now widening with shock. I had caught Monroe off guard.

I continued. "I've seen that look before. That's the look of a man who is in love. I have a feeling that Monroe is in love with you! Monroe, is that right? Are you in love with Bonnie?"

Monroe, now choking back the tears, looked at Bonnie and in his best Texas drawl said, " 'Spect you've always known it!"

Bonnie replied, " 'Spect so!"

Then I said, "And Monroe, look at Bonnie's eyes. I've seen that look as well. That's the look of a woman who is in love."

Bonnie looked at her husband and softly said, " 'Spect you've always known that too!"

Monroe, his voice cracking with emotion, replied, " 'Spect so!"

That was it. The conversation ended there. But in those few moments, Monroe and Bonnie had spoken more words of love than they had shared in decades.

After I left Bonnie's room, I took Monroe out to the back porch for a talk. I said, "Monroe, they tell me that Bonnie hasn't got much time left. In spite of that, you have a golden opportunity just now. You have the opportunity to have a talk with Bonnie. This is your last chance to tell her everything that is on your heart. You can tell her how proud you are to call her your wife. You can tell her what a great job she has done with your children and what a wonderful grandmother she is. Monroe, you have the opportunity to tell your wife how very much you love her and how much you will miss her when she is gone. Don't blow this opportunity!"

I returned for another visit a few days later. When I drove into the driveway, Monroe met me at my car. He seemed animated—for Monroe, that is.

"Well, I did it!" he said.

Startled, I asked, "You did what?"

"I did what you told me to do. I talked to Bonnie, and I told her everything—how much I love her and how proud I am of her!"

"Oh," I said. "How did it go?"

"It went so well that I made all the kids do it too!"

Bonnie died a few days after that, but when she died, this family had no regrets. They had expressed the love they had felt all their life as a family. Their love had become a love expressed before it was too late.

If there are people in your life whom you love, don't wait until the last minute to express your love. Communicate what you feel not just through words but in other ways as well. Communicate your love by your commitment, by demonstrating that you are a person of good character, and by showing tender concern. Do it today! Tomorrow may be too late.

# If you found this book helpful, you'll want to read these other books by Mike Tucker.

## Jesus, He's All You'll Ever Need
*Mike Tucker*

Do you ever yearn for something more? Something better?

Tucker guides you through the biblical book of Luke to give you a close look at Jesus' life. As you read, one thing will become crystal clear. Whatever your needs, whatever your sorrows, whatever your crises, whatever your inadequacies, God has made provision for you. He understands your heart's desire, and He alone can satisfy that desire. He's all you'll ever need.

Paperback, 160 pages.    0-8163-2112-4    US$13.99

## Journal of a Lonely God
*Mike Tucker*

This is the story of God's longing. Read along with Mike Tucker in the book of Genesis about God and His dealings with Adam, Abraham, and Isaac. You'll discover a God who has chosen to take any risk, experience any pain, and suffer any rejection necessary to arrive at unbroken fellowship with you. Reading the stories of the patriarchs is like looking over God's shoulder and peeking at entries in His journal—the journal of a lonely God.

Paperback, 96 pages.    0-8163-2071-3    US$9.99